Canadian Social Studies G

Encouraging Topic Interest

Help students develop an understanding and appreciation of different social studies concepts. Engage students through stories, non-fiction, easy-to-read books, videos, and other resources as a springboard for learning.

Vocabulary List

Students can use the black line master to record new vocabulary of theme related words. In addition, keep track of new and theme related vocabulary on chart paper for students' reference during writing activities. Encourage students to add theme related words. Classify the word list into the categories of nouns, verbs, and adjectives.

Black Line Masters and Graphic Organizers

Use the black line masters and graphic organizers to present information, reinforce important concepts, and to extend opportunities for learning. The graphic organizers will help students focus on important ideas, or make direct comparisons.

Learning Logs

Keeping a learning log is an effective way for students to organize their thoughts and ideas about the social studies concepts presented. Student learning logs also give the teacher insight on what follow up activities are needed to review, and to clarify concepts learned.

Learning logs can include the following kinds of entries:
- Teacher prompts
- Student personal reflections
- Questions that arise
- Connections discovered
- Labeled diagrams and pictures

Rubrics and Checklists

Use the rubrics and checklists in this book to assess student learning.

Table of Contents

ALL ABOUT CANADA
PRINCE EDWARD ISLAND
Maritime Province

www.gov.pe.ca

Capital City: Charlottetown

Main Communities: Charlottetown and Summerside

Provincial Flower: Lady's Slipper

Famous Canadian: Lucy Maud Montgomery (1874-1942) was the famous writer who wrote *Anne of Green Gables*.

Prince Edward Island joined confederation on July 1, 1873 and was named after the father of Queen Victoria of Britain. Found on the east coast of Canada, Prince Edward Island (P.E.I.) is the smallest and only island of the provinces and territories.

P.E.I. and the Micmac people were discovered by Jacques Cartier in 1534. P.E.I. is also the birthplace of Canadian Confederation. Sir John A. MacDonald and his colleagues met in Charlottetown to develop the ideas that would lead to the union of Canada's early provinces into one country.

P.E.I. is 224 kilometres long with many sandy beaches and sand dunes. The Gulf of St. Lawrence surrounds P.E.I. on three sides. People travel to P.E.I. by ferry boat or by crossing Confederation Bridge. Every year, thousands of tourists visit the island to eat lobsters, visit Anne of Green Gables' House and to visit its beaches.

Main industries in P.E.I. include agriculture, tourism, fisheries, and light manufacturing. The red soil of the island produces one of P.E.I.'s major exports: potatoes. Other people in P.E.I. work as Irish moss harvesters. Irish moss is algae. Its extract is used in many products like ice cream, beer, and cosmetics. P.E.I. is also known for lobster, scallops and mussels, oysters, and potatoes.

Brain Stretch:
- Lucy Maud Montgomery has made P.E.I. world famous. Research her name and write a short biography about her life.

All ABOUT CANADA
NOVA SCOTIA
Maritime Province

www.gov.ns.ca

Capital City: Halifax

Main Communities: Halifax, Dartmouth, Lunenburg, Sydney

Provincial Flower: Mayflower

Famous Canadian: Alexander Graham Bell (1847- 1922) was a scientist who invented the telephone.

Nova Scotia was one of the original four provinces to join confederation on July 1, 1867. Nova Scotia means New Scotland, and was first settled by people from Scotland. Nova Scotia has two parts: the mainland and Cape Breton Island. It also has numerous small islands and a rocky coastline.

Cape Breton Island is famous for the Cabot trail. Lunenburg is a UNESCO World Heritage Site and on its waterfront, is the Fisheries Museum of the Atlantic. This Museum celebrates the fishing heritage of the Atlantic Coast of Canada and has an exhibit that contains the world's biggest collection of Bluenose objects. The Bluenose is Nova Scotia's famous schooner pictured on the back of the Canadian dime. Visitors also go the village of Peggy's Cove to see their famous lighthouse.

Some of the main industries in Nova Scotia include manufacturing, fishing, mining, tourism, agriculture, and forestry. In addition, Aquaculture or "fish farming" is a fast growing industry. Some types of "fish farms" include Atlantic salmon, blue mussels, American and European oysters and rainbow trout. In Nova Scotia's Annapolis Valley and in the northern part of the province there are many different types of farms.

Brain Stretch:
- Imagine that you are a lighthouse keeper at Peggy's Cove. What would your daily life be like? Use resources and your own imagination to write a journal entry about your daily routines.
- Research and write a report on the famous Bluenose.

Capital City: Fredericton

Main Communities: Saint John, Moncton, Fredericton, and Bathurst

Provincial Flower: Purple Violet

Famous Canadian: Alex Colville (1920-) is a famous realist painter known for painting wildlife.

New Brunswick was one of the original four provinces to join confederation on July 1, 1867. Originally, Samuel de Champlain and the French settled in what is now called Acadia in 1608. This east coast area is still predominantly French speaking. New Brunswick was named after the royal family of King George III, the house of Brunswick.

The Rocks Provincial Park on the Bay of Fundy is a popular tourist destination in New Brunswick. The Bay of Fundy has impressive tides that rise and fall up to 12 metres in a short time. At Hopewell Rocks large "flower pots" can be seen. These "flower pots" are where the ocean has carved unique shapes from the seabed. New Brunswick is also home to Confederation Bridge, Magnetic Hill and Rocks Provincial Park in the Bay of Fundy.

Main industries in New Brunswick include manufacturing, fishing, mining, forestry service and pulp and paper. Some people also work at bilingual call centres. This is where Canadians call to reach 800 phone numbers for information. Grand Manan is a well-known fishing port in New Brunswick. New Brunswick is also known for growing potatoes and fruit, such as apples, blueberries, strawberries, and cranberries.

Brain Stretch:
- Design a travel poster advertising the many places to visit in New Brunswick.

Visit www.Travel.org/newbruns.html for additional information.

ALL ABOUT CANADA
NEWFOUNDLAND & LABRADOR
Maritime Province

www.gov.nf.ca

Capital City: St. John's

Main Communities: St John's, Corner Brook and Gander

Provincial Flower: Pitcher Plant

Famous Canadian: Christopher Pratt is a famous artist.

Newfoundland and Labrador is the most eastern Atlantic province in Canada. It was the last province to join confederation on March 31, 1949. Newfoundland is an island with Labrador attached to the mainland. The island of Newfoundland has a long rugged coastline and is known as the "Rock". To get to the island, people must fly in on an airplane, or take a ferry.

Newfoundland is famous for its cod fishing and is home to the Grand Banks. The Grand Banks are shallow waters to the east and south of Newfoundland. Some of the richest fishing grounds in the world are found in the Grand Banks. The Vikings were the earliest explorers to Canada, arriving in Newfoundland around 1000 A.D. Later explorers and fishermen traveled across the Atlantic to fish.

Tourists visit Newfoundland for its historical sites, natural landscape, and culture. Whale watching boat tours in coastal waters are very popular and allow people to see humpback whales and other species. Icebergs can be seen most often in the spring and the early summer. Other tourist attractions include the many lighthouses in Newfoundland and Labrador as well as Fogo Island and the East Coast Trail.

Hydro-electricity, mining iron ore, manufacturing pulp and paper and fishing are important industries in Newfoundland.

Brain Stretch:

- Research the Grand Banks and write a report about its importance to Newfoundland and Labrador.

Capital City: Québec City

Main Communities: Québec City, Montreal, Sherbrooke, Hull, and Trois-Rivières

Provincial Flower: White Lilly

Famous Canadian: Pierre Elliot Trudeau (1919-2000) was a famous a Prime Minister of Canada.

Québec is the largest province in Canada and was one of the original four provinces to join confederation on July 1, 1867. The province takes its name from the Algonquin people's word for "the place where the river narrows". In 1534, the explorer Jacques Cartier claimed the land for France and it became a French settlement called New France. Most people in Québec speak French.

Tourists to Québec visit the Citadel in Québec City, the Olympic Park in Montreal, and Québec's many national historical parks. Many tourists also visit Québec City during the famous winter carnival. Montreal is also a popular destination, as it is one of Canada's biggest cities.

Québec is the largest producer of maple syrup in the world. Québec also has more dairy farms than any other Canadian province. Cheeses made in Québec are favourites world-wide and have won many awards. Other industries in Québec include manufacturing, agriculture, electricity production, mining, pulp and paper, meat processing, and petroleum refining. Québec is also known for making paper, boxes, tissue, and newsprint.

Brain Stretch:

- A Québecois inventor named Mr. Bombardier invented the snowmobile in the mid 20th century. Research what other inventions and industries are linked with his name.

- **Capital City**: Toronto, the most populous city in the country

- **Main Communities**: Toronto, Ottawa, Hamilton, London, Windsor, Oshawa, Sudbury, Kingston, Timmins and Thunder Bay.

- **Provincial Flower:** Trillium

- **Famous Canadian:** Sir John A. Macdonald (1815-1891) was Canada's first Prime Minister.

Ontario is the second largest province and was one of the original four provinces to join confederation on July 1, 1867. The name Ontario comes from an Iroquoian word meaning "beautiful lake".

Many tourists visit Ontario to see the CN Tower, Niagara Falls, Kingston's Fort Henry, Moose Factory Island near Moosonee and Algonquin Park. Tourists can also enjoy hiking, rafting, and camping in Ontario provincial parks. Canada's capital city is Ottawa, Ontario, where many people go to visit the parliament buildings. During the winter in Ottawa, people can skate on the world's longest skating rink, the Rideau Canal.

The main industries in Ontario include manufacturing, finance, construction, tourism, agriculture, mining, automotive and forestry. Some people work at federal government offices in Ottawa. Ontario's Niagara fruit belt is known for growing fruit like grapes, peaches and apples.

Brain Stretch:

- Dr. Roberta Bondar, Canada's first female astronaut, was born in Ontario. She went into space in 1992. Pretend that you are a broadcaster and that you are about to interview her for the first time. Write five to ten questions that you would like to ask her.

- **Capital City**: Regina
- **Main Communities**: Saskatoon, Regina, Prince Albert, and Moose Jaw.
- **Provincial Flower:** Prairie Lily
- **Famous Canadian:** Jeanne Sauvé (1922-1993) was a journalist. She was the first female Speaker of the House of Commons and the first woman to become governor general of Canada.

Saskatchewan joined confederation on July 1, 1905 and is one of Canada's Prairie Provinces. Saskatchewan is the only province in Canada to have completely man-made borders.

Early settlers from Europe were encouraged to come to Saskatchewan to farm with the offer of free farmland. Many Métis, Aboriginal peoples, and other people from around the world call Saskatchewan home.

Moose Jaw, Saskatchewan has the largest jet pilot training base in Canada and is home to the Snowbirds. The Snowbirds are military pilots who do tricks with their jets in the air. Saskatchewan also has many national historical parks to visit and is home to the Royal Canadian Mounted Police, Centennial Museum and Chapel.

Saskatchewan's industries include ranching and agriculture, mining, meat processing, electricity production, petroleum refining and services. Saskatchewan is known for it's farming and grows wheat for Canadians and other countries around the world. Saskatchewan is also the largest producer of potash and uranium in the world. Potash is used to help fertilize crops while uranium helps to produce electricity.

Brain Stretch:
- In the 1900s agents traveled to Europe to entice farmers to settle in Saskatchewan by offering free land. Create a poster advertising the free land and good life Canada.

All ABOUT CANADA
BRITISH COLUMBIA
Western Province

www.gov.bc.ca

- **Capital City**: Victoria, located on Vancouver Island
- **Main Communities**: Vancouver, Victoria, Prince George, Kamloops, Kelowna, Nanaimo and Penticton.
- **Provincial Flower:** Pacific Dogwood
- **Famous Canadian:** Emily Carr (1871-1945) is a famous artist from Victoria.

British Columbia joined Confederation on July 20, 1871. It is the most western province located on the Pacific Coast. British Columbia has a mainland and many small islands. These islands include Vancouver Island and the Queen Charlotte Islands. British Columbia has three main landforms: mountains, plains, and plateaus. Half of the province is forested. British Columbia is home to some of the largest and oldest trees in the world.

British Columbia is a popular place for tourists. People visit places like Stanley Park in Vancouver, Whistler and Blackcomb Mountains, Gwaii Haana National Park Reserve, and Yoho National Park.

The industries in British Columbia include forestry, mining, tourism, agriculture, fishing, and manufacturing. British Columbia's Okanagan Valley is well known for growing fruit such as apples, plums, and cherries. British Columbia is also known for developing computer software. The city of Vancouver is often called, "Hollywood North" because many films and TV shows are filmed there.

Brain Stretch:
- British Columbia's ancient trees have been referred to as global treasures. Research these ancient trees and write a report to explain why this is so.

- **Capital City**: Edmonton

- **Main Communities**: Edmonton, Calgary, Lethbridge, Red Deer, Medicine Hat

- **Provincial Flower:** Wild Rose

- **Famous Canadian:** Isapo-muxika (also called Crowfoot) (about 1830-1890) was the peacemaker between his Blackfoot and the rival Cree.

Alberta joined confederation on September 1st, 1905. It was named after a British princess and is one of the Prairie Provinces. The Rocky Mountains are found in this province, but it is also made up of plains.

Calgary and Edmonton are popular tourist destinations. Tourists to Calgary can visit the Olympic Park, the Saddledome, the Glenbow Museum, the Calgary Tower, or attend the Calgary Stampede, a popular annual event. In Edmonton, there is the West Edmonton Mall. This is a huge mall filled with stores, numerous activities and attractions. Edmonton also has Canada's largest living history park, Fort Edmonton Park. Near Edmonton, a 9m tall Easter egg is erected to reflect its Ukrainian heritage. When Alberta visitors go through Banff, they can also visit the Columbia Icefield, Lake Louise and Jasper National Park.

The main industries in Alberta include mining, agriculture, beef ranching, manufacturing, finance, and construction. Alberta is known for growing crops like wheat, barley, and oats. Alberta is the main producer of oil, natural gas, and coal in Canada. Other people work in the technology and research industry. Some people also work as part of the tourism industry.

Brain Stretch:
- Alberta is known as Canada's energy province. Research and explain why Alberta has that nickname.

ALL ABOUT CANADA
MANITOBA
Prairie Province

www.gov.mb.ca

- **Capital City**: Winnipeg

- **Main Communities**: Winnipeg, Brandon, Thompson, Portage la Prairie

- **Provincial Flower:** Prairie Crocus

- **Famous Canadian:** Louis Riel (1844-1885) led the Métis community. He was often called the "Father of Manitoba".

Manitoba joined confederation on July 15, 1870. Its name is a Cree word meaning the "place where the spirit speaks". The Hudson's Bay Company established a trading post in Manitoba in 1670 and many French and British settlers lived in the province early on in Canada's history. The railway brought many settlers to the province to farm its fertile land. Manitoba is home to many Métis, Aboriginal peoples, and other people from around the world. Many people in Manitoba speak English and French.

Churchill, Manitoba, a deep-sea port in Hudson Bay, is the best place in the world to see polar bears that migrate there from the arctic in the wintertime. The Royal Winnipeg ballet is also found in this province. This famous dance company tours across Canada. Tourists, who come to Manitoba, may like to visit places like Clearwater Provincial Forestry Nursery, or Garry National Historic Park.

Main industries in Manitoba include manufacturing, agriculture, meat processing, and mining. The Royal Canadian Mint is in Winnipeg, this is where Canadian coins are made.

Brain Stretch:
- Polar bears are amazing creatures. They have adapted to their environment in order to survive. Use your own knowledge and information from other sources to write a report about the polar bears of Churchill, Manitoba. Is it a place you would like to visit?

www.gov.yk.ca

- **Capital City**: Whitehorse

- **Main Communities**: Whitehorse, Dawson City, Watson Lake
  Old Crow is the only settlement in the Yukon that is north of the
  Arctic Circle.

- **Territorial Flower:** Fireweed

- **Famous Canadian:** Robert Service (1874-1958) is a famous poet.
  He wrote the famous book, Songs of Sourdough.

The Yukon is the smallest of Canada's three territories. On June 13,
1898, the Yukon joined confederation and became Canada's second
territory. The name Yukon comes from a Native word meaning 'great
river'.

In 1896 many people traveled to the Yukon in search of gold. This was
known as the Klondike Gold Rush. By the turn of the century, the gold
rush was over and many people left the area.

The Yukon attracts visitors to explore its natural landscape, and to
witness the Aurora Borealis. Mount Logan is the highest mountain in
Canada and is found in Kluane National Park, within the St. Elias
mountain ranges. The largest non-polar ice field in the world is also
located in the St. Elias mountain ranges. The icefield is 700 metres
and is found deep in the heart of the mountains.

Industries in the Yukon include forestry, construction, manufacturing,
fur trapping, and tourism. The Yukon is recognized for the mining of
natural resources including gold, silver, lead, oil, and zinc. Tourism is
of key importance to the Yukon and provides many service jobs in
hotels, stores, restaurants, outdoor tour companies and transportation.

Brain Stretch:
- What qualities would a prospector during the time of the Klondike
  Gold Rush need to be successful? Use your imagination and other
  resources to fill in the details.

ALL ABOUT CANADA
NORTHWEST TERRITORIES

www.gov.nt.ca

- **Capital City**: Yellowknife
- **Main Communities**: Yellowknife, Hay River, Inuvik and Fort Smith
- **Territorial Flower:** Mountain Avens
- **Famous Canadian:** Georges Erasmus (1948-) is a famous political leader.

The Northwest Territories (N.W.T) is the second largest territory in Canada. It joined confederation on July 13, 1870 to become Canada's first territory. Most of the N.W.T is sub arctic country.

Industries in NWT include services, trapping, mining, forestry, tourism, oil and gas, as well as arts and crafts. The Beaufort Sea and the Mackenzie River delta are areas that are under exploration. Large oil fields lie below these areas and oil companies have been trying to develop the region since the 1970's.

NWT is home to the Mackenzie River, the longest river in Canada, as well as Great Bear Lake, one of the largest lakes in the world. Tourists, who travel to the Northwest Territories, may also be able to witness the Aurora Borealis also known as the Northern Lights. Tourists also like to visit Inukshuks (stone markers) and go to Nahanni National Park.

Brain Stretch:

- Diamond mining has become a very important industry in the Northwest Territories. Why are diamonds so valuable? Use your own knowledge and information from other sources to answer this question in detail.

ALL ABOUT CANADA
NUNAVUT TERRITORY

www.gov.nu.ca

- **Capital City**: Iqaluit
- **Main Communities**: Iqaluit, Rankin Inlet, Arviat and Cambridge Bay
- **Territorial Flower:** Purple saxifrage
- **Famous Canadian:** Peter Pitseolak (1902-19730 was a famous photographer who took pictures of Inuit life.

Nunavut is the newest and largest territory in Canada. It joined confederation on April 1, 1999 and was formed out of the Northwest Territories. Nunavut has many islands, including Baffin and Ellesmere Islands. This area is one of the least populated areas in the world. Most residents in Nunavut are of Inuit descent.

Airplanes are the major source of travel in Nunavut and every community has an airstrip. Airplanes are used to transport people, food, machines or other materials to the areas of Nunavut.

Tourists to Nunavut can experience adventures such as floe edge tours, canoeing, sea kayaking, hiking, backpacking, wildlife, whale watching and other cultural experiences. The Aurora Borealis or The Northern Lights can be observed from Nunavut.

Much of the industry in Nunavut is tourism, hunting and trapping, mining, and fishing. Nunavut is also known for its artists who create fine arts and crafts. Arctic animals such as caribou, polar bears, whales and seals are an important part of the Inuit culture.

Brain Stretch:
- Inukshuks or Inuksuits are Inuit stone towers. Use your own knowledge and other resources to find out more about their importance in Inuit culture and history. Write a brief report.

Province or Territory Quick Review

----

1. This province or territory joined Confederation on

_____.

2. The capital city is

_____

3. Two communities are.

_____   _____

4. Write five facts you learned.

A.
B.
C.
D.
E.

5. If you could visit this province or territory, what would you want to see or do?

_____

_____

_____

_____

Comparing Provinces Or Territories

Compare......		

Canada Activity Cards

ALL ABOUT CANADA
Plan a Vacation

Canada is a vast and diverse country. There are many different places to visit. Research and plan a trip to a province or territory in Canada. What route would you take from where you live? What attractions would you like to see when you get there?

Brain Stretch: Pretend that you are a travel agent and design an itinerary for a trip. Create a travel package that includes:

- An itinerary for your trip with a list of places to visit
- An explanation of why you are traveling to that destination
- Travel tips

In addition, look at the Canada VIA Rail train schedules on the Internet.
www.viarail.com

ALL ABOUT CANADA
Confederation

Canada became a country on July 1, 1867. The name Canada comes from the Huron and Iroquois word "Kanata" meaning "village". When Canada first became a country, there were only four provinces. These provinces were New Brunswick, Nova Scotia, Ontario and Québec. When these provinces joined, it was called Confederation. Over the years, other provinces and territories became a part of Canada. Now Canada has ten provinces and three territories.

Brain Stretch:

- Write the provinces in order from earliest to join confederation to last.

- Visit the following website to learn more about confederation.
  http://www.collectionscanada.ca/confederation/kids/index-e.html

Canada Activity Cards

ALL ABOUT CANADA
Animals of Canada

Canada is famous for its beautiful land and wildlife. The physical regions of Canada are diverse in many ways, including plant life, climate, landforms, natural resources, and animals.

Brain Stretch: Choose an animal from one of the physical regions of Canada. Present your findings in a booklet entitled: "All About the Canadian_____". Research the animal to find information about its:

- Diet
- Habitat
- Adaptation to the region
- Place in the food chain
- Interesting Facts

Important Tip! Make sure to include labeled diagrams and pictures!

ALL ABOUT CANADA
Canada's Rivers And Lakes

Canada's rivers and lakes hold a lot of the worlds freshwater. Freshwater is important because it is good to drink and sustains life.

Learn more about the Great Lakes at the following website:

http://www.ec.gc.ca/grandslacsgreatlakes/default.asp?lang=En&n=70283230-1

Learn more about the importance of freshwater at:
http://www.ec.gc.ca/water/e_main.html

Brain Stretch:

- Make a list of the Great Lakes.
- Make a list of all of the ways water is used in daily life. What would happen if people did not fresh water?
- What is Canada's longest river?

ALL ABOUT CANADA
National Symbols

Canada has several national symbols. Some of these include the Canadian flag, the beaver, and the Royal Canadian Mounted Police.

Brain Stretch: What well-known Canadian symbols are found on these coins?

- penny
- nickel
- dime
- quarter
- loonie
- toonie

- Imagine that you work for the Royal Canadian Mint and that you have been given the task of designing the next coin for Canada. What symbol do you think should be put on the coin? Draw your design.

- Choose a Canadian symbol and explain its significance to Canada.

ALL ABOUT CANADA
Immigration

Every year thousands of people immigrate to Canada. Almost all of the people in Canada can trace their roots back to someone or some people that traveled far to get here. Perhaps you immigrated here also.

Some immigrants apply to become a Canadian citizen. Applications can take a long time to process. If an immigrant meets the requirements to become a Canadian citizen, they take a citizenship test. Once the whole process is finished, an immigrant becomes a Canadian citizen and takes an oath of citizenship at a special ceremony.

Brain Stretch:
- Write a speech entitled, "Canada is the best country in the world to live in". Use your own ideas and other resources to support your position.

- What feelings do you think an immigrant might have coming to a new country?

Canada's Flag

Canada's flag is a red flag with a single, red maple leaf on a white square.

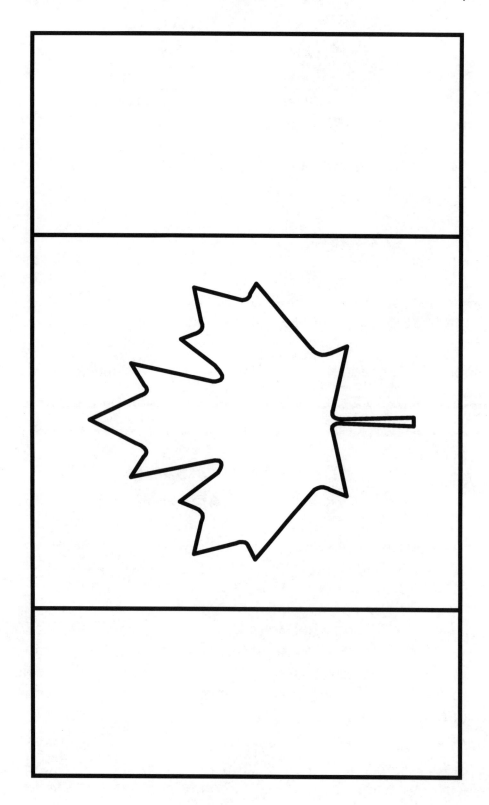

Create A New Canadian Flag

A flag represents a country. A flag is a way for citizens in a country to feel that they belong to the same place. Create your own flag for Canada below.

Write A Canadian Shape Poem

Write a descriptive poem about Canada. Write the poem around the maple leaf.
Draw pictures for your poem inside the maple leaf.

A Political Map of Canada

- Label the provinces and territories of Canada
- Label the Atlantic, Pacific, and Arctic oceans
- Label the capital cities of each province and territory

Provinces And Territories

List Canada's ten provinces and three territories.

Provinces
1.
2.
3.
4.
5.
6.
7.
8.
9.
10.

Territories
1.
2.
3.

Canadian Capital City Match

Match the provinces and territories to the names of their capital cities.

Nunavut	Victoria
Ontario	Halifax
Québec	Fredericton
Alberta	Toronto
Saskatchewan	Winnipeg
Northwest Territories	Edmonton
Nova Scotia	Whitehorse
Newfoundland and Labrador	Québec City
New Brunswick	Regina
Prince Edward Island	St. John's
British Columbia	Iqaluit
Yukon	Yellowknife
Manitoba	Charlottetown

Parent Letter
Provinces and Territories of Canada Project

Dear Parents/Guardians:

Our class is studying the regions, provinces, and territories of Canada. For the next month, the students will be working on a special project, integrating the social studies curriculum with reading, writing, media literacy, and art. They will be collecting information about one province or territory and creating a picture book with the information. They are writing their book with a primary audience in mind.

There are many ways you can help your child. Here are a few:

- ask them about their project and look at the work they are doing

- become a resource to them

- help them use the Internet for research

- discuss newspaper articles about their province or territory

Provinces and Territories of Canada Project

Make a picture book about a province or territory of Canada. Each page must have a picture and information. Here is a list of the information required:

- Cover Page (1 page)

- Capital City (1 page)

- Provincial Flag (1 page)

- Provincial Flower (1page)

- Provincial Bird (1 page)

- Population (1 page)

- Natural Resources (1 page)

- Industry (1 page)

- Attractions or Places to Visit (1 page)

- Famous Person from that Province or Territory (1 page)

Rough copy due date: _____

Good copy due date: _____

Your ongoing support is greatly appreciated!

Sincerely,

Canada's Physical Regions Brochure

Canada has many different physical regions. Each region is very unique. Create a brochure for one of Canada's physical regions. A brochure is a booklet or pamphlet that contains descriptive information. The headings for the brochure are as follows:

- physical features
- climate
- vegetation
- animal life
- natural resources
- interesting facts

STEP 1: Plan Your Brochure

Step	Completion
1. Take a piece of paper and fold the paper the same way your brochure will be folded.	
2. Before writing the brochure, plan the layout in pencil. • Write the heading for each section where you would like it to be in the brochure. • Leave room underneath each section to write information • Also leave room for graphics or pictures	

STEP 2: Complete a Draft

Step	Completion
1. Research information for each section of your brochure.	
2. Read your draft for meaning and then add, delete or change words to make your writing better.	

STEP 3: Final Editing Checklist

I checked for spelling _____   My brochure is neat and organized _____

I checked for punctuation _____   My brochure has pictures or graphics _____

I checked for clear sentences _____   My brochure is attractive _____

Medieval Times Cards

MEDIEVAL SOCIETY
Feudal Life

The king was the head of medieval society. All of the land belonged to the king. In this "feudal" system, the king awarded land grants or "fiefs" to his most important nobles, barons, and bishops. In exchange, the nobles supported the king and provided soldiers for the king's army.

The king and queen held court and listened to petitions made by their people who needed help. The king or queen had advisors to help make decisions. The king or queen also made proclamations about the rules of the kingdom and taxes.

Brain Stretch:

- If you were a king or queen, what proclamations would you make to keep your subjects happy?

- Do you think a good king or queen has to keep his subjects happy? Explain your thinking.

MEDIEVAL SOCIETY
Nobles

Nobles were under the king and queen in the medieval society hierarchy. Most nobles had titles such as duke, count, earl, margrave or marquis. Most lords and ladies lived in manor houses which were quite large and made of stone. Manor houses usually had great halls or rooms to host celebrations and meetings.

Nobles, who had been granted large estates, divided their land into three parts. Each year only two thirds was farmed. The remaining third would be left fallow for a year. The farmed land would be divided into strips to divide among the serfs of the manor. Serfs, also known as peasants, would farm the land for the nobles. Some portion of the crop would be given to the church.

Brain Stretch:

- Why do you think the nobles didn't farm all of the land each year?

- Why is it beneficial to leave a portion of the land fallow? Use research and your own ideas to answer this question.

Medieval Times Cards

MEDIEVAL SOCIETY
Freemen

Freemen and women worked for money. Some were craftspeople, and others were farmers. Freemen were free to move around and work where they wanted. They paid rent and taxes to the lord of the manor or king. There were many types of jobs in a village, such as: weaver, reeve, blacksmith, joiner, baker, miller, shepherd, apothecary, butcher, entertainer, furrier, thatcher, mason, musician, and doctor.

Brain Stretch:

- Choose one of the freemen jobs and write a job advertisement for it. What would the advertisement say?

- Look at classified ads in a newspaper to help you with the format of the ad. Make sure that you include what skills and characteristics are needed for the job. Also include an address where the applicants can go to for an interview.

MEDIEVAL SOCIETY
Serfs

A serf or peasant had very few possessions. They would spend their entire lives working on a manor for a nobleman, only leaving with permission from the lord of the manor. A serf or peasant, would farm the noble's land for half the week. He would then have the rest of the week to farm a plot of land for his family. Some of his crop would be given to the nobleman in taxes and to the church. The rest would be used to feed his family and perhaps sell for a small amount of money. A peasant's cottage was a simple one-room building made of wood or clay. The floor was dirty and there was an open fire to cook and keep warm. The roof was made of thatched straw.

Brain Stretch:
- Use your own ideas and information from other sources to compare your home with that of a peasant in the Middle Ages. How are they the same? How are they different? Display your results in a Venn diagram.

Medieval Times Cards

MEDIEVAL SOCIETY
Knights

Most lords of manors were also knights. When there was a war, the lords were away fighting with their army. During times of peace, they looked after their land and practiced their skills at battle. They would check on their farms daily and ensure that taxes were paid properly. Knights swore allegiance to the king. Knights would often practice their skills by taking part in competitions, like: jousting and archery. Sometimes these competitions were big festivals in the kingdom.

Brain Stretch:

- Using information from other sources and your own ideas make a character sketch of a knight.
- What kind of characteristics did knights have to be successful? Find as many adjectives as you can to describe your knight and explain why you chose those particular words.

MEDIEVAL SOCIETY
Knight Poetry

Poetry was common in medieval times. Write a cinquain poem about a knight. Use some of your words from your previous character sketch to help you.

A cinquain poem has five lines:

1st line – one word (Knight)
2nd line – two adjectives describing line one
3rd line – three verbs related to line one
4th line – a four word phrase about line one
5th line – a synonym for line one

Medieval Times Cards

MEDIEVAL SOCIETY
Weaponry

Knights were very brave and went to battle when called upon by the king. They were accompanied by brave men who were loyal to the king. Several types of weapons were used in battle: mace, swords, lances, battle axes, arrows and the trebuchet. To defend themselves, they used shields, chain mail, armour, and castles were fortified with stone walls.

Brain Stretch:

- Research a tool or weapon that was used in the Medieval Ages. Use your own ideas and other sources to write a brief description for each.

- Create a model of your chosen weapon and put it on display for your class.

MEDIEVAL SOCIETY
Becoming A Knight

Young boys dreamed of becoming a knight in medieval times. Only the sons of noblemen could choose this path. The boy would leave his home at seven years of age and live at the castle as a page. A page served and ran errands. At nine, the boy became a valet who served the knight and ran errands for the ladies. When he turned fifteen, the lad would become a squire. A squire followed a knight everywhere and helped him whenever required.

Brain Stretch:
- Pretend that you are Merlin, the advice columnist. Use your own knowledge and other resources to write a response to Linus.

Dear Merlin,
      I am a young lad wishing to pursuit knighthood. I want to be brave in battle, but I don't like following orders. What steps should I take to make my dream a reality? Do you think I have what it takes to be a knight?

Yours,
Linus

Medieval Times Cards

MEDIEVAL SOCIETY
Education

Very few people could read and write in medieval times. The priest was usually the only person who was able to teach children. Noble and freemen families usually paid for their sons to have some education before learning their father's trade or becoming a page. Girls were rarely educated. Girls were usually trained to learn their mothers' skills and were often put in a convent to become a nun.

Brain Stretch:

- What do you think about the unequal treatment of girls and boys in medieval society? Explain your thinking.

- Do you think girls and boys are treated differently in society in the 21st century? Explain your thinking.

MEDIEVAL SOCIETY
Justice

The lord of the manor made the rules for his estate. Whenever someone was caught in a dispute or breaking the rules, they would be brought to the court held in the manor house. There were no prisons, and justice was often harsh for serious crimes. English Common Law was developed from the common rules of society that were generally accepted as right. People in medieval times agreed with what was right and what was wrong. Canadian law is based on many English Common Law principles.

Brain Stretch:
- What common rules does your classroom have? Do you agree with them? Is there a rule that you would add to the list?

Medieval Times Cards

MEDIEVAL SOCIETY
Magna Carta

The Magna Carta or "Great Charter" was signed by King John of England. The noblemen of the time insisted upon it. This charter changed medieval society and the power of the crown. The charter ensured that:

a) No one would be imprisoned without a trial

b) Standard weights and measures would be established

c) The church can appoint who it wants to church positions

Brain Stretch:
- Choose one of the points above and write a persuasive paragraph to support or disagree with it.

MEDIEVAL SOCIETY
Castles

The castle was a very important part of medieval society. It was the home of the king and queen, and the centre of a kingdom. Castles were usually built with surrounding walls for security. However, when canons were invented making it easy for attackers to destroy stone fortifications, walls were built less often. Many people lived within the castle walls and others lived in the country surrounding the fort.

Brain Stretch:

- Use what you already know about castles and do further research to develop your understanding. Design a castle plan.
  Include: A wall, moat, village houses, and farms in your map.
  Turn it into a 3-D version.

Medieval Brain Stretch Activities

MEDIEVAL TIMES CARD
Create A Menu

Create a menu for a medieval feast and a menu for a modern day feast.

- Compare the two menus and explain how they are the same and different.

- Which menu do you prefer? Explain your thinking.

MEDIEVAL TIMES CARD
Write an Article

Choose one of the topics listed below and write an article for the Crusades Chronicle. Try your best to be accurate and research your article.

- A day in the life of a serf
- A knights dilemma
- Women's work in medieval times

MEDIEVAL TIMES CARD
Write an Acrostic Poem

Write an acrostic poem with the word MEDIEVAL.

MEDIEVAL TIMES CARD
Rebus Brain Stretch

A rebus is a sentence or paragraph that has pictures or symbols in place of words or phrases.

- Write your own rebus paragraph about medieval times. Ask a friend or your teacher to read it aloud to you.

MEDIEVAL TIMES CARD
Create a True & False Quiz

Use your knowledge and other resources to write 10 true statements about medieval times and 10 untrue statements about medieval times.

- Test you teacher and friends with your ideas.

MEDIEVAL TIMES CARD
Write a Diary

Travel in time and choose a role. Become a king, queen, serf, knight, lady or lord. Write a diary about what life is like in medieval times.

Medieval Brain Stretch Activities

MEDIEVAL TIMES CARD
Medieval School

Boys and girls were educated very differently in medieval society.

- If you were the principal of a medieval school, what subjects would you make your students study?

- What would they have to learn to be successful?

MEDIEVAL TIMES CARD
Noble Advice

A young noble boy was sent to live in the castle and work as a page. His parents wanted him to become a knight. He however wanted to be a stonemason.

- What advice can you give him?

MEDIEVAL TIMES CARD
Design Stained Glass

Stained glass was very popular in Medieval cathedrals and castles.

- Design a stained glass window depicting a medieval scene. Your pencil line will be the leaded parts, so make them dark and 1 cm thick.

MEDIEVAL TIMES CARD
The Plague or Black Death

The Plague or Black Death killed about one million people during medieval times. It wiped out entire communities!

- Use your own ideas and research to compare the plague with a modern disease.

MEDIEVAL TIMES CARD
Salt

Salt was highly valued in medieval society. Only lords and kings had it on their table. Their guests could use it.

- Use your own ideas and other sources to find out why salt was so precious.
- Explain your findings and compare them to how we value salt today.

MEDIEVAL TIMES CARD
Wanted Poster

Robin Hood is a well-known character from medieval times that lived in the forest with his merry men. He stole from the rich to give to the poor.

- Design a wanted poster for Robin Hood. Imagine that you are the lord responsible for catching him. Draw his picture and use words and phrases to describe his personality.

Create A Shield

Heraldry is a system of symbols on a shield or coat of arms used to represent a noble family. Colour and design was a very important way to indicate family ties. Use the template below to design your family shield. On a separate piece of paper, write about the symbols and colours you used, explain why you used them.

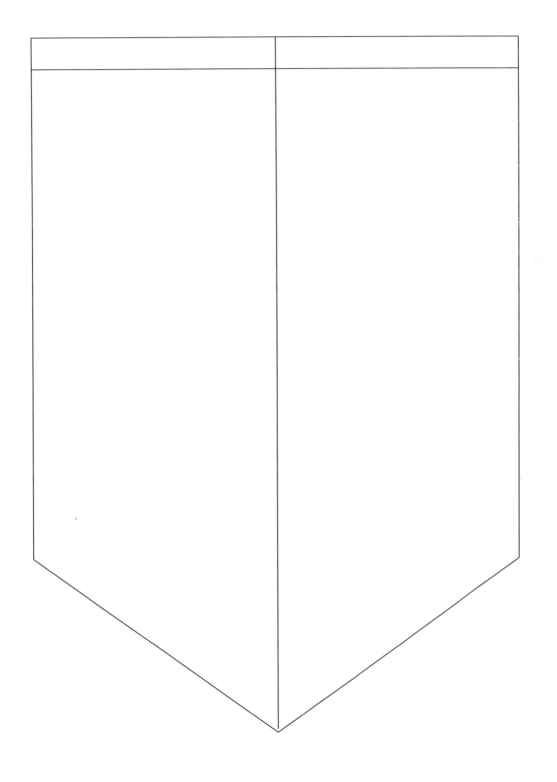

Medieval Society True or False Quiz

name _____

Indicate if the statement is true or false.

Statement	T	F
1. A serf could work towards being a knight.	T	F
2. A serf farmed his own plot of land.	T	F
3. Manor houses were made of stone.	T	F
4. The Magna Carta gave the king the right to imprison anybody.	T	F
5. Children were better educated in medieval times than now.	T	F
6. Many lords were also knights.	T	F
7. A king paid taxes to his noble knights	T	F
8. Knights would win prizes at tournaments	T	F
9. Thatched roofs were common.	T	F
10. Serfs farmed all the land in a manor each year.	T	F
11. A mace is a club–like weapon	T	F
12. Castle walls acted as a prison to keep people in.	T	F
13. Freemen could work for money and travel wherever they wanted	T	F
14. Robin Hood worked for King John.	T	F
15. Salt was a highly valued spice.	T	F

Number correct: _____

CANADIAN GOVERNMENT
Confederation

The Dominion of Canada was formed on July 1, 1867. Dominion is the word to describe a self-governing nation within the British Commonwealth. When Canada first became a country in 1867, there were only four provinces that joined: New Brunswick, Nova Scotia, Ontario, and Québec. The provinces joined together because they believed that this would make them stronger, both militarily and financially. Since then, six more provinces and three territories have joined.

The British North America Act is a document which states how the Canadian government should work. In 1982 the Constitution Act was created, including the BNA act and all other written rules for the country.

Brain Stretch:
- The politicians responsible for Canada's Confederation are often referred to as the "Fathers of Confederation". Find out more about one or more of these people and why they thought Confederation was necessary.

- What benefits would a province have from joining other provinces in confederation? What would they have to sacrifice in order to join?

CANADIAN GOVERNMENT
Canada's Government

The term constitutional monarchy, describes countries that still have a king or queen as the symbolic head of state, but the people elect the government. Canada is a constitutional monarchy that is organized on a federal system of government. Other countries that have a federal system government are the United States of America, Australia and Switzerland.

In Canada, the federal system of government is organized so that powers and responsibilities are divided between the federal government stationed in Ottawa and each of the provincial and territorial governments. Also, every city or smaller community has a local government called a municipal government. Municipal governments have specific responsibilities too.

Brain Stretch:
- Do you agree that Canada should still have a British monarch as its head of state? Choose yes or no and write a persuasive paragraph in support of your position.

Canadian Government Cards

CANADIAN GOVERNMENT
The Governor General

The Governor General is the British Monarch's representative in Ottawa. He or she lives in a beautiful home called Rideau Hall. It is the grandest of all political residences in Canada. The Governor General is selected by the Prime Minister and then appointed by the sovereign. This appointment lasts from five to seven years.

The Governor General has a very ceremonial role in parliament, such as: giving new laws royal assent or approval, appointing new superior court judges, dissolving Parliament, and also inviting a political party with the most support to form the government. Each parliamentary session begins with a speech from the Throne by the Governor General. Other duties include: hosting royal visitors and other important visitors to Canada, presenting medals for bravery and other awards and traveling to other countries to represent Canada.

Brain Stretch:

- At least two of our Governor Generals have been visible minorities as well as immigrants to Canada. Why is this significant for Canada?

- What is the, "Order of Canada"? Research and explain.

CANADIAN GOVERNMENT
Federal Government

The Federal Government of Canada is seated in Ottawa, Canada's capital city. The government works and meets in the Parliament Buildings. The Governor General is the leader of the government, but works under the advice of the Prime Minister. The federal government is responsible for things such as: citizenship, trade, defense, criminal law, Aboriginal Affairs, money, transportation, the postal service and foreign relations with other countries.

The Federal Government of Canada has three parts:
- The Legislative Branch (House of Commons and Senate)
- The Judiciary Branch (Supreme court and other courts)
- The Executive Branch (Prime Minister and his/her cabinet)

Brain Stretch:
- The Federal Government of Canada is responsible for establishing good relationships with other countries. The U.S.A. is our closest neighbour. Do you think that it's important that Canadians and Americans get along? Explain why.

CANADIAN GOVERNMENT
House of Commons

The House of Commons is a group of 301 elected Members of Parliament (MP). They represent all of the communities across Canada. Each representative has a seat in the House and meets with the group to debate issues and pass laws. The political party with the most MPs elected to the house, becomes the party in power and forms the government. That party's leader then becomes the Prime Minister. The party with the second highest number of seats becomes the Opposition and its head becomes the Leader of the Opposition. The Speaker of the House acts as a referee and ensures that the MPs follow parliamentary rules. All of the MPs speak to parliament through the Speaker of the House.

Brain Stretch:

- There are more than ten official political parties in Canada. Use your own knowledge and other resources to list them. Choose one that you would like to learn more about and write a summary of their policies.

CANADIAN GOVERNMENT
Parliament Buildings

The Parliament Buildings of Canada are found in Ottawa, our nation's capital. Queen Victoria chose Ottawa as the capital even though she had never been there, because it appeared to be in the centre of the country. Ottawa, in fact, is on the border of Ontario and Québec.

The Parliament Buildings are made up of an East Block, a West Block and Centre Block. The Centre Block also contains the Library and the Peace Tower. The first building was destroyed by fire in 1916. The current structure, except the Peace Tower, was completed in 1922. The Library of the Parliament was the only part that survived the original building. It contains thousands of precious books. A huge Canada celebration is held on the front lawn of the Parliament buildings on Canada Day.

Take a virtual tour of the buildings at:
http://www.parliamenthill.gc.ca/text/explorethehill_e.html#3

Brain Stretch:
- Why do you think the Parliament Buildings so magnificently designed?

CANADIAN GOVERNMENT
Supreme Court

The Supreme Court is a part of the Judiciary Branch of Government in Canada. It is the highest court in the land. The Supreme Court only considers cases that interpret laws and acts passed by different levels of governments to ensure that they follow the Charter of Rights and the Constitution.

The Supreme Court is made up one Chief Justice and eight other justices. The meet in January, April, and October. It makes judgments on cases, as well as advises the federal and provincial governments about issues related to the constitution. The Supreme Court building is a very impressive building in Ottawa.

Brain Stretch:

• Have you ever considered becoming a judge? What would be challenges might a judge face in doing his/her job?

• Who is the chief justice of Canada's Supreme Court Today?

CANADIAN GOVERNMENT
Provincial and Territorial Governments

In general, provinces and territories are responsible for issues related to education, health and welfare, property, civil rights, justice, and natural resources.

The Lieutenant Governor of the provinces and the Commissioner of the territories are the heads of this level of government. They act on the advice of the Premier or Government Leader. The territories were created through federal law and differ from provinces in three ways. First, the crown land is still held by the federal government. Second, the federal government can get involved in territorial affairs. Last, the territories do not have a vote in constitutional matters.

Brain Stretch:
• Who is the Premier or Government leader of your province or territory?
• Who is the Lieutenant Governor?
  Use your own knowledge and other sources to find out what issues are important to them.

Canadian Government Cards

CANADIAN GOVERNMENT
Municipal Government

Municipal governments are local governments. A municipal government works in partnership with provincial and federal governments. To become a municipality a community must have three things: official city or town limits or boundaries, a council to make decisions on behalf of local residents, and ways to carry out decisions for the good of the community.

Most local governments elect a leader, called a mayor. The mayor is the chair of the elected council. Council members along with other elected officials make decisions to help a community run smoothly. During council meetings there are debates about how to spend money, how to provide public transportation or ideas on how to make the community a better place to live. In general, the responsibilities of a municipality include: managing water, sewage, waste collection, public transit, emergency services, animal control, land planning, libraries, and economic development.

Brain Stretch:

- What does your municipality do with its garbage?   Write a letter to the head of your municipality summarizing your findings.

- Describe the characteristics of a good mayor. Explain your thinking.

CANADIAN GOVERNMENT
Prime Minister

The Prime Minister is usually a Member of Parliament who is the leader of the political party that holds the majority of seats in the House of Commons. The Governor General appoints the Prime Minister. The Prime Minister selects his or her Cabinet from members of his or her political party. The Cabinet helps the Prime Minster make decisions about how to run the country. The Prime Minister speaks for the government of Canada and represents Canada in international relations. The Prime Minister lives at 24 Sussex Drive in Ottawa. This manor house sits on a cliff in view of the Parliament Buildings.

The biggest and most difficult task for the Prime Minister is to try to make sure the concerns of each of the provinces and territories is met. The Prime Minister has an important role in meeting with their leaders to discuss topics of concern to the whole country. Meetings with these leaders are called First Ministers Conferences.

Brain Stretch:
- Who is the Prime Minister today? Imagine that you are a newspaper reporter about to interview the Prime Minister. Write ten questions that you plan to ask.

CANADIAN GOVERNMENT
How Laws Made Are Made

The Legislative Assembly is where ideas are presented and made into laws. Laws first begin as ideas, and then ideas become bills. A bill is a rough draft explaining the idea behind the law. The legislative process is the special procedure where bills can become laws or acts.

Creating a law is just like the process of writing. Once the need for a new law is determined, its wording is carefully studied and crafted A bill has a first reading in the House of Commons to inform the members of parliament. During the second reading of the bill, members of parliament discuss and debate the advantages and disadvantages of the proposed law. Then, the bill is sent to a Standing Committee related to the topic for further review. A Standing Committee is made up of MPs from all of the parties to ensure that all sides are considered. The Standing Committee reports back to the House of Commons and suggests amendments if necessary. Further debate happens during the third reading and it is voted on for the last time. Once a bill has been voted on three times, it must be approved by the Senate and signed by the Governor General.

Brain Stretch:

• How are rules made at your school? How should they be made? Write a persuasive letter to your teacher or principal on the topic of school rules.

CANADIAN GOVERNMENT
Green Government Challenge

Imagine that the Prime Minister of Canada has just appointed you Minister of the Environment. You know that the citizens and voters of Canada are becoming increasingly concerned with global warming, climate change, air pollution and water pollution. This is definitely going to be a major issue in the next federal election.

Your Task:

1. Research the environmental issues that concern Canadians.

2. Find out what causes these environmental problems.

3. Devise a plan to address these issues and improve the environment

4. Write a paper outlining: A "Green Plan" to improve Canada's environment. This should be written as a persuasive paper.

The Charter of Rights & Freedoms

The **Charter of Rights and Freedoms** is an important document found inside Canada's Constitution Act, 1982.

Canadians have the "right" to do certain things in everyday life without government intervention. Some of the "rights" guaranteed for Canadians include:

"Right"	What It Means
Canadians have the "right" to vote for their own government once they are of age.	Canadians can choose any candidate of their choice to vote into an elected office.
Canadians have the "right" to run for elected office.	This means Canadians can enter a race to become an elected official.
Canadians have the "right" to have freedom of speech.	This means Canadians can freely state their opinions even if they don't agree with the government.
Canadians have the "right" to freedom of religion.	This means Canadians can belong to any religion they choose, or not belong to any religion.
Canadians have the "right" of freedom of association.	This means Canadians can belong to any group or organization they choose.
Canadians have the "right" of movement.	This means Canadians can travel throughout Canada without the government's permission.
Canadians have the "right" to a fair trial if arrested or accused of a crime.	This means Canadians can't be kept in jail without being proven guilty.
Canadians have the "right" to be treated equally under the law.	This means all people are treated the same, no matter who they are.

Brain Stretch:

1) Using information from the reading and your own ideas, explain which three "rights" are the most important for Canadians.

2) If Canadians did not have "rights", what kind of place would Canada be like to live? Explain your thinking.

The Government In Our Daily Life

Almost every part of our daily life is some way influenced or controlled by the Canadian government. This is because the government has three very important responsibilities: to provide services, create laws, and to make sure the laws are clear.

Research different sources such as government web sites, or look up government departments in the telephone book and fill in the chart below.

Examples of Federal Government Services or Departments	Examples of Provincial Government Services or Departments	Examples of Municipal or Local Government Services or Departments

Canada's Links To The World Cards

Canada's Links to the World
Natural Resources

Canada is a country rich in many natural resources. Use an atlas to find at least ten natural resources and list at least one way that each is used. Create a chart such as the following.

Natural Resource	Use

CANADA'S LINKS TO THE WORLD
Imports and Exports

Canada is a country that depends on trade. Trade happens in two ways: exports and imports.

Exports are goods that are for sale or exchange to other countries. Some of Canada's major exports include aluminum, precious metals and metal ores, newsprint, lumber, wood pulp, wheat, natural gas, petroleum, and technology.

Imports are goods that a country purchases or trades for from other countries. Countries import items from other countries around the world for several reasons. They may not be able to produce or grow the item, like oranges. Or another country might be specialists at producing some specific product. Sometimes it may actually be easier to buy a product from another country than make it themselves. Some of Canada's major imports include cars and car parts, fruits and vegetables, and technology.

Brain Stretch:
* Make a list of products are imported to Canada and exported from Canada. Who are Canada's major trading partners?

Canada's Links To The World Cards

CANADA'S LINKS TO THE WORLD
Gross Domestic Product

A country's Gross Domestic Product or GDP is a measure of all of the goods and services produced in that country during one year. It is generally used to measure the size of a country's economy. If the GDP is growing, it is then believed that a country is doing well. If the GDP is decreasing, it is believed that a country is going through some economic difficulty. Usually this means more unemployment and a lower standard of living for the citizens of that country.

Brain Stretch:

- Do you think a government in power should be judged by the GDP? Use your ideas and other sources to write a response.

- What is Canada's GDP?

CANADA'S LINKS TO THE WORLD
North American Free Trade Agreement

Canada signed the North American Free Trade Agreement (NAFTA) with the United States and Mexico in 1994. This created the world's largest free trade area and created a new bond with Canada's closest neighbours.

NAFTA has created a lot of controversy in Canada and the other countries involved. Some big corporations believe that NAFTA is a good idea because it lowers the taxes paid on exports, which increases their profits.

On the other hand, some labour unions are against NAFTA because they believe that the agreement will take jobs away from Canadians and give the work to countries that pay their workers less money. Some farmers and politicians are also concerned with the agreement. Several disputes have arisen between the countries, dealing in the trade of natural resources, such as softwood lumber.

Brain Stretch:

- Which side are you on? Do you support NAFTA or are you opposed to it? Use your own ideas and other sources to support your position.
- Complete a T-chart to list the pros and cons of NAFTA using information from resources and your own ideas.

CANADA'S LINKS TO THE WORLD
Celebrating our Heritage

Canada is a diverse nation, rich in culture and heritage. Different ethnic groups have immigrated to this country, bringing with them new languages, foods, celebrations, religions and traditions.

Rather than abandon their roots, these ethnic groups share their culture with the rest of Canadian society. Often this is in the form of heritage celebrations, such as Caribana or Chinese New Year. These celebrations are an example of how other countries have influenced contemporary Canadian society.

Brain Stretch:
- Create a collage depicting the different influences made by cultures in Canada. You can include: food, dress, language, dance, etc.

CANADA'S LINKS TO THE WORLD
Canada's Influence in the World

Canada has produced many influential people and inventions.

Banting and Best, two researchers in Toronto, invented Insulin which helps people with diabetes lead normal lives. Hockey was invented in Canada and is now played in many countries around the world. Spar Aerospace designed the Canadarm which acts as an external arm on space shuttles. There are many, many more important Canadian inventions.

Brain Stretch:

- Use your own knowledge, books and other sources to choose a Canadian invention or idea that has impacted the world. Create a poster, including a detailed picture and information, about the invention or idea.

A Famous Canadian

Complete a timeline of the significant events in the life a famous Canadian.
Use the graphic organizer to help you.

Name _____

I chose this famous Canadian because…

_____

_____

_____

Date	**Event**

A Famous Canadian

Name _____

Date	Event

Canada's Imports and Exports

Fill in the charts below by finding the following:

- 5 products that are exported from Canada to other countries.
- 5 products from around your home or school such as clothing or food items that are imported from other countries.

Canada's Exports

Product	Country of Origin

Canada's Exports

Product	Country Exported To

What surprised you in your findings? Explain your thinking.

Canada's Natural Resources

Canada is rich in natural resources. This is considered natural wealth. Some of Canada's natural resources are forestry, hydroelectricity, mining, oil, gas, agriculture, and fishing.

Why must Canada care for its natural resources? Explain.

Compare Canada and _____

Comparing....	Canada	
What is the population?		
What is the area?		
What is the official language?		
What is the capital city?		
What is the system of government?		
What are the bordering countries?		
Currency		
GDP		
Natural Resources		

Canada's Trading Partners Research Assignment

Choose a country that has a trading relationship with Canada. Research the country using the Internet, encyclopedias and books to provide the following information:

1. Name of Country:

2. Geographical Information:

- How is the country divided
- Capital city
- Population
- Map

3. Political Information:

- Name of the political leader
- Official languages
- Flag
- History information (e.g. independence)

4. Economic Information:

- Natural resources
- Main Industries
- Main exports and imports

5. Other Information

After gathering research from a number of sources and taking notes, present your findings using your own words. Whenever possible, use original artwork rather than borrowed pictures from the internet. Choose a booklet, brochure or scrap book format to present your work.

First Nations and Explorers Cards

FIRST NATIONS AND EXPLORERS
Bering Land Bridge

During the last ice age, when the Northern Hemisphere was covered in ice, the Bering Strait was turned from liquid to solid. This joined what is modern day Russia with Alaska. This is a popular theory of how humans came to live in North and South America. The theory suggests that the bridge allowed people and animals to migrate from Asia to North America. These groups of humans would have been nomadic hunting tribes following herds of animals.

Brain Stretch:

- On a map of the world, locate: Asia, North America, South America and the Bering Strait. Use a dotted line to show the migratory route suggested in this theory.

FIRST NATIONS AND EXPLORERS
Creation Stories

We know of the Bering Land Bridge theory regarding how humans got to the Americas. Creation stories are also very well known explanations for how people came to live here. All of Canada's Aboriginal groups have their own creation stories.

Brain Stretch:

- Read a creation story from one of Canada's aboriginal groups. Retell it in your own words and draw a symbol to represent the story.
- Create your own version of a creation story.

First Nations and Explorers Cards

FIRST NATIONS AND EXPLORERS
Aboriginal Groups

Canada is a very large and diverse country with seven different physical regions. First Nations tribes in Canada, and around the world, adapted to their environment. They established very close relationships with the environment in which they lived.

Every aspect of First Nations' culture, including: religion, housing, clothing, food, transportation, was influenced by the environment and region in which it developed. Some of the Aboriginal cultures are: Northwest Coast, Cree, Plains, Plateau, Innu, Inuit, Iroquoian, Algonquin, and Micmac.

Brain Stretch:

- Use your own knowledge, textbooks or other sources to label as many different First Nations tribes on a map of Canada.

FIRST NATIONS AND EXPLORERS
Explorers

Visit this website to find an extensive list of explorers with pictures, route maps and historical significance.

http://www.civilization.ca/vmnf/explor/explcd_e.html

Brain Stretch:

- Pick and explorer and write a biography about them.
- Map out their route.
- What do you think are the characteristics of an explorer? Explain.
- Would you want to be an explorer? Explain.

First Nations and Explorers Cards

FIRST NATIONS AND EXPLORERS
Housing

Housing styles vary from country to country, and physical region to region. The same was true for the First Nations groups in Canada. Northwest Coast tribes lived in plank houses; tribes in the arctic made igloos, the Plains tribes lived in teepees and the Algonquin in wigwams. Iroquoian tribes made longhouses. Each shelter was made from resources found in the local environment and suited the climate.

Brain Stretch:

- Research and create a model of a First Nations shelter.
- Write a brief description of it.
- How is it the same and different to where you live?

FIRST NATIONS AND EXPLORERS
Clothing

First Nations traditional clothing was similar to modern clothing. It was practical, yet often very beautifully made. In most tribes, women were responsible for making clothing for their families. Animal skins and fur were used, as were quills and decorative shells and beads when available. All tribes would have seasonal clothing to keep them protected from all of the elements.

Brain Stretch:

- Look at an example of First Nations clothing and an example of your shoes.
- Make a sketch of both.
- Write a description for each.
- Use a graphic organizer to compare them.

First Nations and Explorers Cards

FIRST NATIONS AND EXPLORERS
Hunting, Gathering, Farming and Fishing

The environment was extremely important to all of the First Nations tribes. Their very subsistence depended on their ability to get food. Some tribes were hunters and gatherers, others were farmers, and some relied on fishing.

Brain Stretch:
- Imagine that you are a young First Nations person. Which tribe would you have like to belong to? Explain your thinking.

FIRST NATIONS AND EXPLORERS
Transportation

The First Nations people invented different methods of transportation that are still used in modern times. Horses are not native to North America and were brought to Canada by Europeans. Early tribes traveled on water or walked to their destination. "Kayak" and "canoe" are native words for two different types of boats.

Brain Stretch:

- Use your own knowledge and other sources to find out the similarities and differences between kayaks and canoes. How are they made? Where were they used? Show your findings using a Venn diagram.

First Nations and Explorers Cards

FIRST NATIONS AND EXPLORERS
Totem Poles

Totem Poles are animal symbols that represent an Aboriginal Canadian family or clan. These symbols were used in different parts of the country. In 1701, the Great Peace of Montreal was signed by many different chiefs from warring Aboriginal Nations to put an end to their conflict. Each chief signed the agreement with a picture of their family or clan totem. Totem poles are unique to six West Coast First Nations. They carved giant cedar trunks with the animal symbols of their family members, clansmen and storytelling.

Learn more about Totem poles at the following website:

http://indigenousfoundations.arts.ubc.ca/home/culture/totem-poles.html

Brain Stretch:

- After you have read more about totem poles design a totem pole to represent yourself. What animal will represent your spirit?

FIRST NATIONS AND EXPLORERS
Women and Men at Work

Historically, women and men in all societies have had different roles and jobs. In early First Nations groups, the roles of women and men were also distinct, yet equally important. First Nations people worked and lived with their family members. Everyone had an important job to do to keep the family healthy and safe.

Brain Stretch:

- Research and use a graphic organizer to compare what work First Nations women would have been responsible for and what work First Nations men had to do.

First Nations and Explorers Cards

FIRST NATIONS AND EXPLORERS
Government

The Iroquois Confederacy was a famous union of First Nation groups. These tribes were the Mohawk, the Oneida, the Onondaga, the Cayuga, and the Seneca. Later on, a sixth tribe the Tuscarora also joined. The Iroquois Confederacy is often credited with influencing the democratic systems of government in both Canada and the United States of America. They were often referred to as the "League of Peace and Power"; the "Five Nations"; the "Six Nations"; or the "People of the Long house".

Brain Stretch:

- What system of government did other First Nations have? Choose one from the Northwest Coast, Inuit or Plains or Cree to research. Write a brief summary of their system of governance.

- Do you think it was a fair system? Explain your thinking.

- Why were the Iroquois Confederacy known as the "People of the Long house"?

FIRST NATIONS AND EXPLORERS
Vikings

It has long been understood and accepted that the Vikings were the first to visit what we now know to be Canada.

The Viking Sagas were stories told about Erik the Red and Lief Erikson. However, for a long time these stories were thought to be fictional. In the last half of the 20th Century, maps of Leif's voyages and actual archaeological evidence was found to support the idea that he and some of his peers were actually on Canadian soil in approximately 1000 A.D. This makes them the first Europeans to find the New World.

The Viking archaeological site at L'Anse aux Meadows, in Newfoundland, is a UNESCO World Heritage Site. It is the only known Viking site in North America.

Brain Stretch:
- A world heritage site is a place that The United Nations Educational, Scientific and Cultural Organization (UNESCO) considers to be of outstanding value to humanity. Why do you think that the L'Anse aux Meadows site was chosen to be a world heritage site? With research to support your answer, write an article about this early Viking settlement.

First Nations and Explorers Cards

FIRST NATIONS AND EXPLORERS
European Explorers

European countries rushed to sponsor brave explorers willing to go to sea to find undiscovered lands. Originally, Europeans were in search of spices, such as pepper, cinnamon, cassia, nutmeg, cloves and ginger. They rushed to find a quick route to the East (India, Sri Lanka, and China). After the New World was discovered, the Europeans wanted to claim it for themselves. They also wanted control over the fur trade and fisheries.

Brain Stretch:

- Using a map of the world, and a legend, use lines to show the voyages of at least three different European explorers.

- Do you think the European explorers were being greedy? Explain your opinion.

FIRST NATIONS AND EXPLORERS
Reasons for Exploration

European countries like, Britain, France, and Spain had different reasons for wanting to explore new lands. In most cases, there was a sense of urgency to get to new lands first and claim them for their own. Some went in search for spices and silk, while others were off to the New World to claim land for their king.

Brain Stretch:

- Imagine that you are a crewmember on a famous explorer's ship. Write a diary entry about a day in the life of your adventures. Remember to use what you know and other sources to make your entry realistic and descriptive.

First Nations and Explorers Cards

FIRST NATIONS AND EXPLORERS
Technology for Exploration

New technologies made it possible for explorers to travel farther from home. In the middle of the last millennium, several new inventions helped guide explorers to the New World, including: the astrolabe, rudder, latten, cross-staff and compass.

Brain Stretch:

- Check out the website below to see Samuel de Champlain's Astrolabe. Draw a sketch of an astrolabe and write a brief description of how it helped him arrive in the New World.

http://www.civilization.ca/tresors/treasure/222eng.html

FIRST NATIONS AND EXPLORERS
Newspaper Analysis

Canadian First Nations have had many difficulties due to European exploration, settlement and influence. A lot of recent First Nations issues have dealt with health care issues, land claims and restitution for past wrongdoings by government agencies.

Issues related to First Nations peoples in Canada are often in the newspapers. Too often these articles deal with negative or tragic stories, rather than celebrate First Nations culture and success stories.

Brain Stretch:
Read the newspaper for a week or two and collect newspaper articles about issues related to the First Nations people of Canada.

a) Summarize the article

b) Write a reflection or response to the article with particular focus on whether it is a positive or negative view of First Nations people.

First Nations and Explorers Cards

FIRST NATIONS AND EXPLORERS
Importance of the Environment

Aboriginal people have always had a very close relationship with their environment. All aspects of their culture were influenced by their surroundings, including: food, clothing, transportation, shelters, pastimes, and religious beliefs.

Brain Stretch:
- Choose one of the Aboriginal groups and outline how the environment influenced their culture.

FIRST NATIONS PROJECT

First Nation:_____

Your group is responsible for create a scrapbook about the First Nations People named above. Your scrapbook should include the subtopics listed below. Each group member is responsible for one of the subtopics. Once all of the written work is complete, create a model, diorama, to display with the scrapbook. In addition, make sure to add artwork to the scrapbook

Subtopic	Author	Editor
Housing		
Diet		
Transportation		
Women's Work		
Men's Work		
Spirituality		
Clothing		
Recreation		

EXPLORERS OF CANADA
Poster Assignment

1. Choose an early Canadian Explorer. There are a few names at the bottom of this page to choose from.

2. Research the person you have selected. Record your information in a web like the following

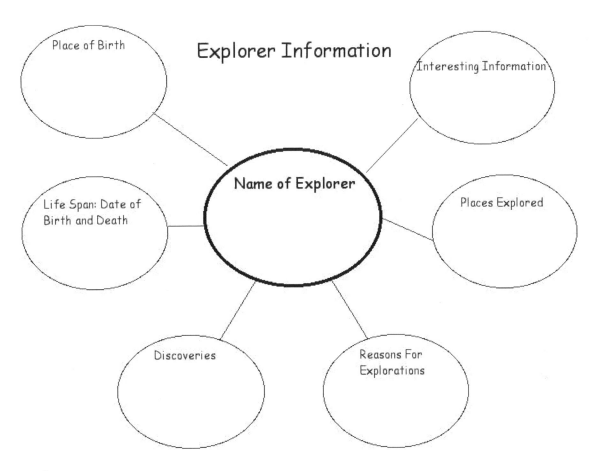

Explorer Information

Place of Birth

Interesting Information

Life Span: Date of Birth and Death

Name of Explorer

Places Explored

Discoveries

Reasons For Explorations

3. Create a poster that includes a picture of your explorer and symbols or written notes that represent the information in your web.

Giovanni Caboto	Simon Fraser	Alexander McKenzie
Jacques Cartier	Martin Frobisher	George Vancouver
Samuel de Champlain	Samuel Hearne	Leif Erikson
John Franklin	Henry Hudson	David Thompson

A Famous Explorer

Complete a timeline of the significant events in the life a famous explorer. Use the graphic organizer to help you.

Name _____

I chose this famous Canadian because...

_____

_____

_____

Date	Event

A Famous Explorer

Name _____

Date	Event

Show What You Know Challenge

First Nations and Explorers of Canada

1. How important was the environment to First Nations people? Explain.

2. Name at least two contributions made by early aboriginal people to modern Canada.

3. How did the physical region affect the diet of a First Nation group? For example, how did living in the arctic affect the diet of the Inuit people?   Explain and give examples.

4. Explain one theory about how First Nations people came to what is now Canada.

5. What is a totem?

6. How did work differ for men and women in First Nations groups?

7. How did contact with Explorers and European settlers affect First Nations people?

8. What issues face First Nations in Canada today?

9. Who is credited with being the first European explorer to discover Canada?

10. What technologies made exploration of the New World possible?

11. What did the European explorers want to get in India and the East?

12. When they discovered the New World, what resources were they looking for?

Create an Ancient Civilization Magazine

Congratulations!

You have been selected to create a new magazine about an ancient civilization!

A **civilization** is a group of people with an organized and technologically advanced culture. In ancient times, there were many different groups of people who lived in different parts of the world. Some of these groups became very successful and powerful and still influence modern day life. For example:

- Did you know that many English words come from ancient Greek language?

- Did you know that acupuncture was invented in Ancient China?

- Did you know Ancient Egyptians invented "papyrus", a paper like material for writing?

- Did you know that the Ancient Maya invented one of the first calendars?

- Did you know that the Ancient Romans were master builders?

Step One: Let's get started!

Choose one of the following ancient civilizations to base your magazine on.

- ❖ Ancient Greece
- ❖ Ancient Rome
- ❖ Ancient China
- ❖ Ancient Maya
- ❖ Ancient Egypt
- ❖ Other _____

List your group members:

Create An Ancient Civilization Magazine

Step Two: Become an expert historian!

Usually historians look at four categories of information when learning about a culture. Use the chart below to help organize your magazine into 4 parts. Make sure to include all the writing topics in your magazine.

Environment

How did the surrounding air, land and water influence the ancient civilization?

Article Topics:

- ❑ landforms
- ❑ climate
- ❑ vegetation
- ❑ natural resources
- ❑ bodies of water

Social Life

How did people relate to each other?

Article Topics:

- ❑ social structure
- ❑ family
- ❑ language
- ❑ education
- ❑ religion
- ❑ arts
- ❑ sports and recreation

Political Life

How did the people make decisions together as a group?

Article Topics:

- ❑ political structure
- ❑ defence and war
- ❑ government and citizenship
- ❑ the legal system

Economic Life

How did people meet their physical needs to survive?

Article Topics:

- ❑ food and farming
- ❑ homes
- ❑ trade
- ❑ technology
- ❑ health
- ❑ clothing
- ❑ occupations

Here is an excellent website to help gather information for your magazine.

http://ancienthistory.mrdonn.org/indexlife.html

Step Three: Assign Jobs for Group Members

Step Four: Write Drafts and Edit

Create An Ancient Civilization Magazine

Step Five: Magazine Checklist
Here is a checklist for a top quality magazine.

Magazine Cover

☐   The title of the magazine is easy to read and prominent on the cover

☐   There is an attractive illustration to let readers know the theme of the magazine.

☐   There are 1 or 2 magazine highlight statements about what is inside the magazine.

Editor's Page

☐   The letter is addressed to the readers.

☐   The letter lets readers know why you think it is important to study an ancient civilization.

Table of Contents

☐   There is a complete listing of what is in the magazine.

Advertisements

☐   There are student-created advertisements throughout the magazine such as for occupations and community events that relate to the ancient civilization.

Magazine Articles

☐   All the jobs on the magazine plan are complete.

☐   Environment Section

☐   Social Life Section

☐   Political Life Section

☐   Economic Life Section

☐   Point of View

Visual Appeal

☐   The magazine has neat and colourful hand drawn pictures, maps and other labeled diagrams.

Other article ideas and columns to include in your magazine:

- Important Inventions
- An interview with a citizen
- Architecture

- Biography of a famous citizen
- Retelling of a myth or legend
- Interesting facts

Magazine Plan

Group Members: _____

Job	Group Member	Complete

Magazine Article Checklist

These are the parts of an article you need to know:

- The **HEADLINE** names the article.
- The **BYLINE** shows the name of the author. (You)
- The **BEGINNING** gives the most important idea.
- The **MIDDLE** gives supporting details about the idea.
- The **ENDING** usually gives the reader an idea to remember.

Article Checklist:

Content

- ☐ I have a **HEADLINE** that names the article.
- ☐ I have a **BYLINE** that shows my name as the author.
- ☐ I have a **BEGINNING** that gives the most important facts.
- ☐ I have a **MIDDLE** part that tells details about the article.
- ☐ I have an **ENDING** that gives the reader an idea to remember.

Grammar and Style

- ☐ I used my neatest printing and included a clear title
- ☐ I included a colourful picture to support my article
- ☐ I spelled my words correctly
- ☐ I used interesting words
- ☐ I checked for capitals, periods, commas and question marks

Take One Point Of View

Write an article that gives your point of view about an ancient civilization. Use this outline to plan your article

- Ancient civilizations have influenced modern day life.

A Statement Of Your Point Of View	
Assertion	Supporting Evidence
Assertion	Supporting Evidence
Assertion	Supporting Evidence

Magazine Rubric

Group Members _____

Project: _____

Criteria	Level One	Level Two	Level Three	Level Four
Content/Information • information • accuracy • supporting details	-limited information -few supporting details	- some of the required information - some supporting details	- most of the required information - accurate and complete supporting details	- comprehensive information - very thorough supporting details
Writing Conventions • spelling • grammar • punctuation	spelling and grammar errors in good copy - inconsistent punctuation	- some spelling, grammar, and punctuation errors in good copy	- most of the spelling, grammar and punctuation is correct in good copy	- all spelling, grammar, and punctuation are correct in good copy
Graphics / Pictures • match information • colour enhanced	- pictures rarely match information - incomplete	- pictures partially match information - some pictures are incomplete	- pictures are complete and appropriate	- pictures are outstanding and consistently match information
Overall Presentation • neat • organization	- little organization or neatness	- some organization and neatness	- general organization and neatness	- outstanding organization and neatness

Teacher Comments:

ARTIFACT ASSIGNMENT

Ancient Civilization Museum Curator

As a museum curator it is your job to bring the most interesting artifacts from history to the public and present them in clear and thought-provoking ways.

Step One
Choose an artifact from an Ancient Civilization such as weaponry, housing, clothing, writing or tool and research it.

Step Two
- Create a picture or sketch of the artifact.

Step Three
Conduct research and collect information as to the artifact's significance in that civilization. For example:

- What was its purpose?
- What did it look like?
- How was it made?
- Who used it?
- What does it tells us about that civilization?

Create a brochure or paper outlining this information. This description will accompany your artifact and explain it to the viewing public.

STEP 3: Final Editing Checklist

I checked for spelling _____   My brochure is neat and organized _____

I checked for punctuation _____   My brochure has pictures or graphics _____

I checked for clear sentences _____   My brochure is attractive _____

PLAN A TRIP TO AN ANCIENT LAND

Congratulations!

You have won an all expenses paid trip for you and your family to visit the historic sites of any ancient civilization. You can choose from:

- Ancient Maya
- Ancient Greece
- Ancient Egypt
- Ancient Rome
- Ancient China

In order to have your trip fully funded, you must provide our tour company, Ancient Travel with a detailed itinerary. It should include:

➤ A labeled map of your chosen destination.

➤ Detailed descriptions of all of the ancient sites that you would like to see, including pictures and written descriptions.

➤ An approximate timetable for each day of the week long ancient civilization experience.

➤ A postcard that you would like to send back to friends. It should be a picture of a famous ancient site on one side and a brief description on the flip side.

Present your itinerary in a neat and clear way. Package your itinerary creatively and send it to us as soon as possible! Don't delay!

A website to visit for great information on ancient lands is:
http://www.historyforkids.org/

Comparing Ancient Civilizations

Comparing…..		

Ancient Civilizations Brain Stretch Activities

ANCIENT CIVILIZATIONS
Slavery

Most of the Ancient Civilizations practiced slavery. Slaves performed many different roles: household chores, nannies, trades, and more.

- Travel back in time and interview a slave. Compose 10 questions to ask them. Put yourself in their position and write their responses to your questions.

ANCIENT CIVILIZATIONS
Biography Poster

Research a famous citizen from an ancient civilization and write a biography.

- Why do you think people are still so interested in this person?

ANCIENT CIVILIZATIONS
Modern Day Comparison

Use a graphic organizer to compare and contrast daily life in an ancient civilization with modern day life.

Possible Comparisons:

- Occupations
- Clothing
- Sports and Recreation
- Housing

ANCIENT CIVILIZATIONS
Gods and Goddesses

All of the Ancient Civilizations had strong religious beliefs and values. Many of them worshipped several different gods.

- Research a god or goddess from an ancient civilization. Find out why they were worshipped. Write a letter or prayer to them in the role of an ancient nobleman or noblewoman.

ANCIENT CIVILIZATIONS
Clothing

In ancient times the clothing a person wore helped to show where they were from, if they were rich or poor and if they were male or female.

- Research the clothing worn in an ancient civilization.

- Design an outfit that might have been worn in ancient times. Write an explanation to go with it.

ANCIENT CIVILIZATIONS
Architecture

Ancient civilizations built magnificent buildings, monuments and structures. Examples include: the Egyptian Pyramids, the Greek Acropolis, the Roman Arch of Constantine, and the Great Wall of China.

- Research an example of ancient architecture and create an advertisement to encourage people to visit it.

Canada Quiz

Use the words in the word bank below to complete the following statements.

1. _____ is the smallest province in Canada.

2. _____ joined Canada in 1999.

3. The official languages of Canada are _____ and _____.

4. The capital city of Canada is _____.

5. Four provinces joined to form Canada in the year_____.

6. Mt. Logan, Canada's highest peak is in the __ _____.

7. The _____'s picture is on the dime.

8. Cape Breton Island is a part of _____.

9. _____Bridge is connects New Brunswick to P.E.I.

10. The CN Tower is in _____.

11. _____ is the largest province.

12. There are 10 _____ and 3 _____ in Canada.

13. The Royal Canadian Mint is in _____.

14. Victoria is B.C.'s capital city and it is found on _____island.

15. Dinosaur Provincial Park is found in _____.

Word Bank

Québec	English	French	Yukon	P.E.I	Ottawa
Nunavut	Ontario	Bluenose	1867	provinces	Vancouver
territories	Alberta	Manitoba	Nova Scotia	Winnipeg	

Medieval Times Quiz

name _____

Use the words in the word bank below to complete the following statements.

1. Some farmland was left _____ each year to let it recover.

2. Kings and Queens lived in _____ that were usually fortified.

3. The _____was a very important document that has influenced modern society.

4. The _____was the head of the church.

5. Serfs worked on the land owned by the _____.

6. Knights practiced their _____ & _____.

7. _____law was established to keep order in medieval society.

8. Heraldry was very important. Noble families would display their _____to show their family ties.

9. _____ were workers who were paid for their work.

10. Many houses were made out of _____and _____.

11. A very contagious and deadly disease is called a _____.

12. A _____was a man who made tools and objects from metal.

13. A noble boy who served a lord and lady was called a _____.

14. Many houses had _____roofs.

15. _____were wars waged to control the Holy Lands.

Word Bank:

Magna Carta	page	castles	Pope
coat of arms	thatched	freemen	wattle
jousting	common	daub	plague
blacksmith	fallow	archery	crusades
nobles			

Canadian Government Quiz

name _____

Use the words in the word bank below to complete the following statements.

1. The Dominion of Canada was formed on July 1, _____.

2. Canada's head of state is the _____.

3. The three levels of government in Canada are: _____ ,
    _____ and_____.

4. The _____represents the monarch in Canada.

5. The federal government meets in the _____buildings.

6. There are 301 elected representatives in the House of _____.

7. The _____ Tower was built in 1922.

8. The Supreme Court is made up of one _____Justice and eight other
    justices. They meet three times a year.

9. _____are the heads of territorial governments.

10. Sewage, waste collection and libraries are the responsibility of the
    _____governments.

11. The _____ lives at 24 Sussex Drive.

12. Agnes McPhail was the first _____Member of Parliament.

13. Canada's first Prime Minister was _____.

14. Provincial leaders are called _____.

15. Queen _____ chose Ottawa as Canada's capital.

Word Bank:

governor general	monarch	Parliament	municipal
1867	chief	commons	John A. MacDonald
peace	federal	Prime Minister	commissioners
provincial	local	premiers	female
Victoria			

Ancient Civilizations Quiz

name _____

Use the words in the word bank below to complete the following statements.

1. The _____ River runs through Egypt and was an important part of ancient Life.

2. The _____ were held every four years to honour Zeus.

3. The Ancient Mayans and Egyptians built magnificent _____. These structures were often the _____ for dead nobles.

4. _____ were used to transport trade goods and weapons.

5. _____ , _____ and _____ are believed to be the first kinds of crops grown.

6. The _____ stone is a tablet that translated several ancient languages.

7. The Ancient Egyptians wrote using _____.

8. _____ were at the top of Ancient Egyptian society.

9. The _____Sea is the body of water found between

Greece and Egypt. Merchants often sailed across it to _____ goods.

10. All Ancient societies had some form of _____. They often believed in many different gods.

11. In Ancient times boys were often better _____ than girls.

12. _____ were used to perform daily household duties.

Word Bank:

pharaohs	slaves	pyramids	tombs
corn	Olympics	Mediterranean	boat
educated	spirituality	Rosetta	trade
hieroglyphics	beans	squash	Nile

Canada's Links To The World Quiz

name _____

Use the words in the word bank below to complete the following statements.

1. _____ are goods that a country makes that it sells to other countries.

2. Canada has a rich _____ industry. Iron and nickel are _____ resources found in Canada.

3. The _____ is Canada's greatest trading partner and closest neighbour. It has fifty _____.

4. Sir Sandford _____ is a famous Canadian who invented the idea of standard time and _____

5. _____ are goods that a country trades for or purchases from other countries.

6. All of the goods and services produced in a country in one year is measured by its _____.

7. Canada's rich heritage is due in part to the many _____ who make it a diverse country.

8. _____ is the capital city of the U.S.A.

9. _____ is a trade agreement between Canada, U.S.A and _____.

10. Countries often _____ goods to get things that they cannot make or that are cheaper. Most imported goods are charged a tax called a _____ when they enter the country.

Word Bank:

exports	imports	natural	trade
GDP	NAFTA	Fleming	time zones
immigrants	U.N.	U.S.A.	mining
Mexico	Washington	states	tariff

Canada's First Nations and Explorers Quiz   name _____

Use the words in the word bank below to complete the following statements.

1. The _____ are believed to be the first Europeans to discover Canada at about 1000AD.

2. One theory states that Canada's First Nations' ancestors came across the _____ Land Bridge from what is now known as Russia.

3. West Coast aboriginal groups made _____ poles to show their family history and to tell family stories.

4. European explorers originally were in search of a route to the Far East because they wanted to get _____ and _____.

5. Once the New World was discovered, European explorers wanted to trade with the First Nations for _____. They also wanted to _____ off the coast of Newfoundland.

6. The _____ was very important to First Nation groups. It influenced the clothing, housing and culture of the people.

7. The _____ and _____ were two inventions that made early exploration possible.

8. Canada's First Nations lived in houses, like: _____ and _____.

9. Jacques _____ explored Canada in 1534.

10. Some First Nations groups traveled by _____ or _____.

11. Inuit groups built _____ to show the way for travelers.

Word Bank:

Bering	totem	fish	environment
fishing	canoe	longhouses	wigwams
Inukshuk	vikings	Cartier	astrolabe
compass	spices	silk	fur

Answers: Canada Quiz

1. PEI
2. Nunavut
3. French, English
4. Ottawa
5. 1867
6. Yukon
7. Bluenose
8. Nova Scotia
9. Confederation
10. Ontario
11. Quebec
12. Provinces, territories
13. Manitoba
14. Vancouver
15. Alberta

Answers: Medieval Times Quiz

1. fallow	2. castles	3. Magna Carta
4. Pope	5. nobles	6. jousting, archery
7. common	8. coat of arms	9. freemen
10. wattle, daub	11. plague	12. blacksmith
13. page	14. thatched	15. Crusades

Answers: Canadian Government Quiz

1. 1867	2. Queen	3. Federal, Provincial, Municipal
4. Governor General	5. Parliament	6. Commons
7. Peace	8. Chief	9. Commissioners
10. Municipal	11. Prime Minister	12. female
13. John A. MacDonald	14. Premiers	15. Victoria

Answers: Ancient Civilizations Quiz

1. Nile	2. Olympics	3. pyramids, tombs
4. Boats	5. corn, beans, squash	6. Rosetta
7. hieroglyphics	8. pharaohs	9. Mediterranean
10. spirituality	11. educated	12. slaves

Answers: Canada and Its Links to the World Quiz

1. exports	2. mining, natural	3. U.S.A. , states
4. Fleming, time zones	5. imports	6. GDP
7. Immigrants	8. Washington	9. NAFTA, Mexico
10. trade, tariff		

Answers: First Nations and Explorers Quiz

1. Vikings	2. Bering	3. totem
4. silk, spices	5. fur, fish	6. environment
7. astrolabe, compass	8. wigwams, longhouses	9. Cartier
10. canoe, kayak	11. inukshuk	

What I think I know...

What I wonder about...

New Vocabulary

Vocabulary Word	Definition

Non-Fiction Reports

Encourage students to read informational text and to recall what they have read in their own words. Provide a theme related space or table, and subject related materials and artifacts including, books, tapes, posters, posters and magazines etc.

Have students explore the different sections usually found in a non-fiction book:

The Title Page: The book title and the author's name.

The Table of Contents: The title of each chapter, what page it starts on and where you can find specific information.

The Glossary: The meaning of special words used in the book.

The Index: The ABC list of specific topics you can find in the book.

Next, discuss criteria of a good research project. It should include:

- a presentation board or other medium
- proper grammar and punctuation, for example, capitals and periods
- print size that can be read from far away
- neat colouring and detailed drawings

Oral Reports

Encourage students to talk about what they have learned and to make a presentation to the class. Here are tips to discuss with students.

- Use your best voice, speak slowly, and make sure your voice is loud so everyone can hear.
- Look at your audience and try not to sway.
- Introduce your topic in an interesting way (Riddle, or Question).
- Choose the most important things to tell.
- Point to pictures, a model, or diorama, as you present.

Blooms Taxonomy in the Classroom

Knowledge: (recall)

- *Activities:* match, describe, identify, name, select, and define.
- *Products*: timeline, a facts chart, make a list
- *Ask questions such as:* What are the definitions of _____?
  Can you name the _____?

Comprehension: (understanding)

- *Activities:* explain, predict, summarize, classify, and sort.
- *Products*: cartoon strip, draw a picture
- *Ask questions such as:* Why do you think…?
  What are the differences?
  Explain your thinking with an example

Application: (using information)

- *Activities*: rearrange, solve problems, modify, and demonstrate.
- *Products*: mural, make a scrapbook, diorama, dress up as___
- *Ask questions such as:* What questions would you ask?
  Can you group by characteristics such as?
  Could this have happened in _____?

Analysis: (studying the components)

- *Activities*: order, estimate, subdivide, infer, separate
- *Products*: family tree, construct a graph to show the information, prepare a report
- *Ask questions such as:* Can you explain what must have happened when ___?

  How is _____similar to _____?
  What are some of the problems of _____?

Synthesis: (creating a whole from parts)

- *Activities:* design, create, compose, combine, rearrange, construct
- *Products*: Design a t-shirt, write a story
- *Ask questions such as:* Draw _____.
  Create a model that shows _____.
  How could you make ____?

Evaluation: (making judgements)

- *Activities:* justify, categorize, conclude, support, compare
- *Products: write a letter, make a booklet and convince others of your ideas*
- *Ask questions like:* What solution did you like best? Why?
  What was the best/worst thing about _____?
  Which ____ did you like? Why?

Create A Stamp

Write about your stamp.

Write A letter

Dear _____

_____

_____

_____

_____

_____

_____

_____

_____

_____

_____

_____

_____

Your friend,

A Flip Book

Make a flip book about your topic of study using outline pages. Fold the sheet along the dotted line. Next, cut the sheet along the dark solid lines. Answer the question on the outside page, and draw a picture to go with it on the inside page.

Compare and Contrast

Compare to look at what things are the **same**.
Contrast to look what things are **different**.
Find two things, people, events or ideas to compare and contrast.

Compare
How are they the **same**?

Contrast
How are they the **different**?

A Collage About _____

Find pictures or words from magazines, newspapers or other sources about your topic. Cut and paste them into a collage.

An Advertisement For

_____

A Venn Diagram About _____

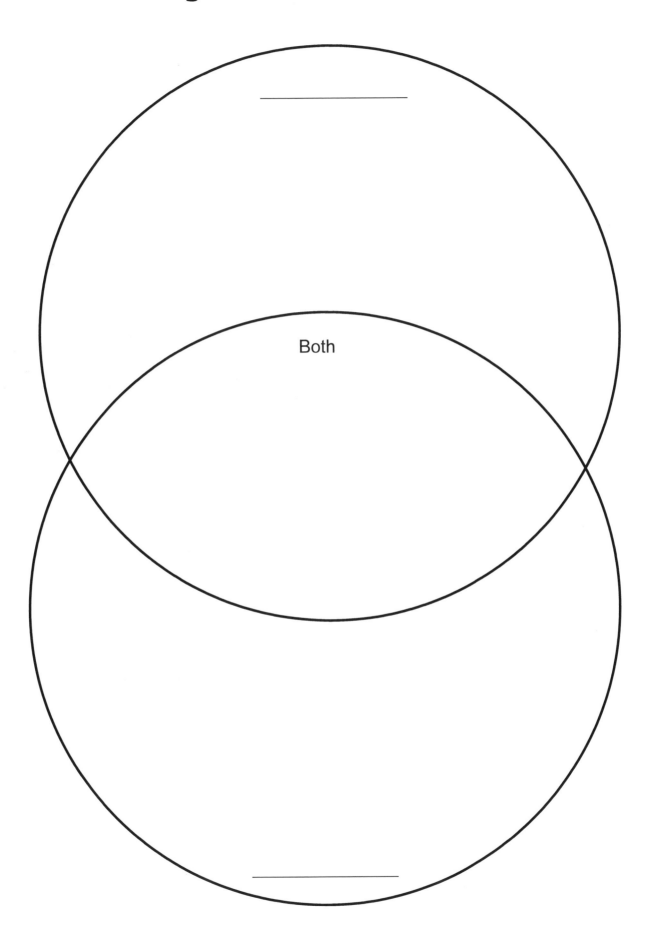

Both

A Web About _____

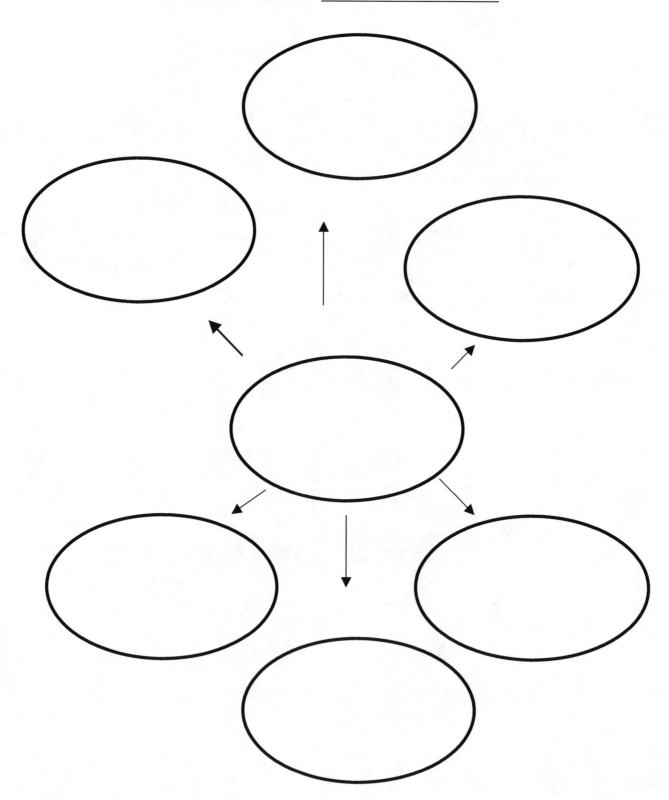

Comparison Chart

name _____

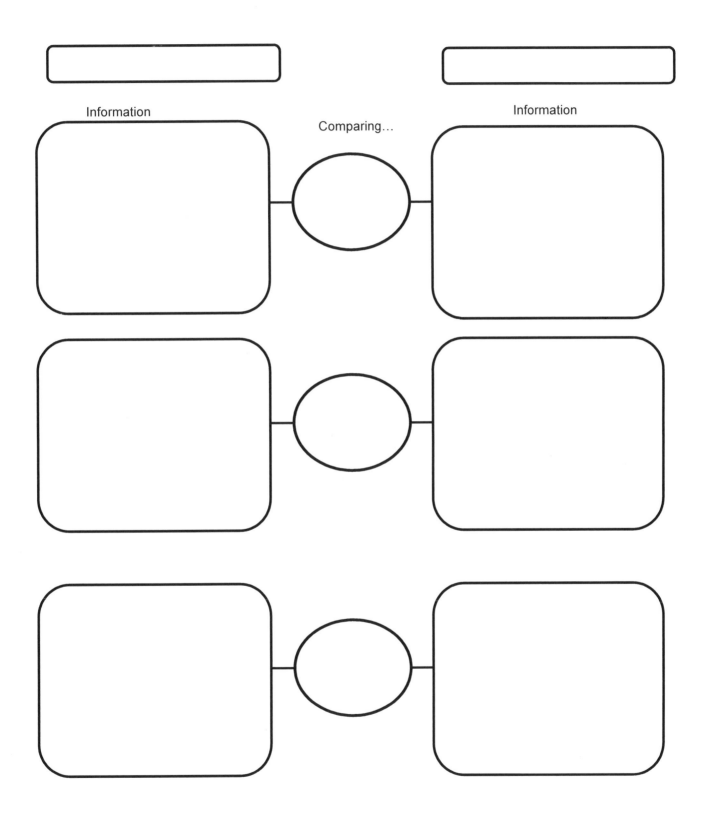

Information

Comparing…

Information

Conduct a Survey

name _____

This is a graph about _____

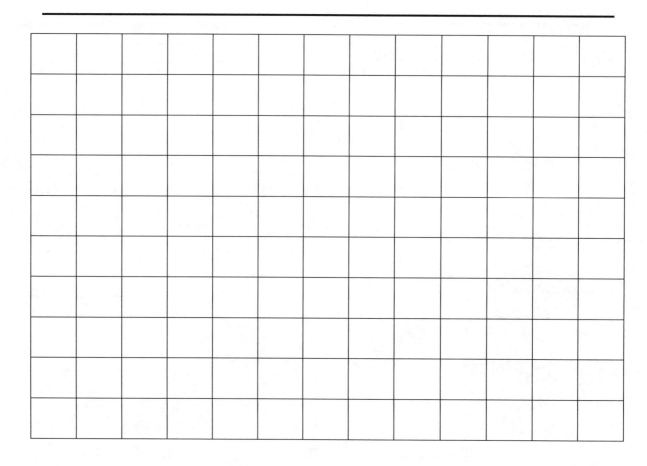

By looking at the graph, I learned that:

_____

_____

_____

_____

_____

A POST CARD

Front of Postcard

Back of Postcard

To:

A T-Chart About _____

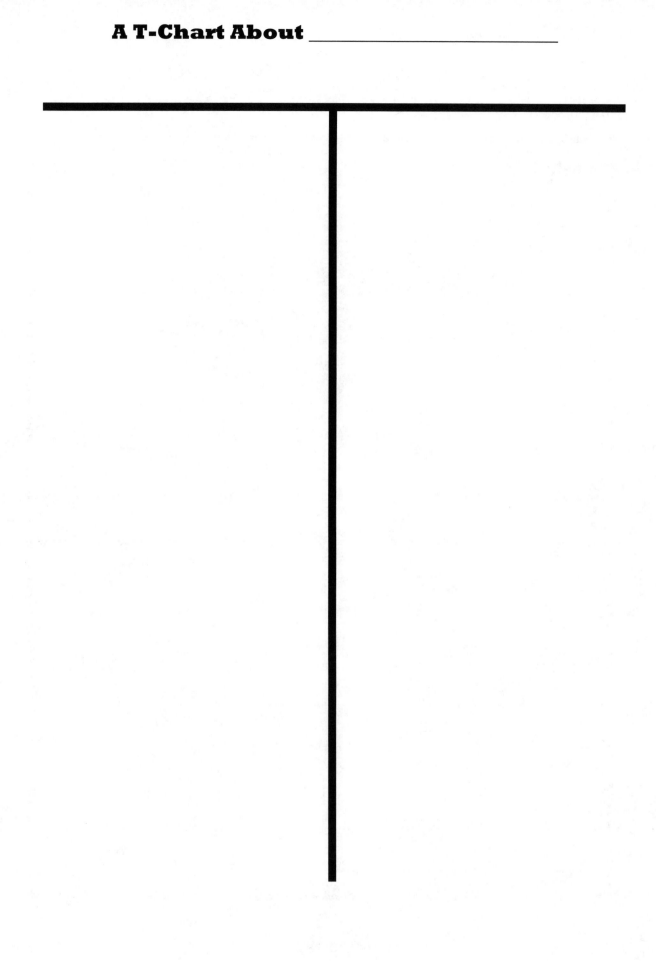

What I Wonder...

This is a map of ____________________________________

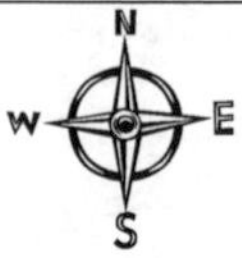

Legend

A Comparison of _____

Comparing…..		
Who?		
What?		
Where?		
When?		
How?		

Write a News Story

Pretend you are a newspaper reporter and a write a news story.

Here are the parts of an article.

- The **HEADLINE** names the story.
- The **BYLINE** names the author.
- The **BEGINNING** tells the reader the most important idea.
- The **MIDDLE** gives details about the story.
- The **ENDING** gives the reader an idea to remember.

Newspaper Article Checklist:

Grammar and Style

- ☐ I used my neatest writing and included a clear title.
- ☐ I included a colourful picture.
- ☐ I checked for spelling.
- ☐ I used interesting words.
- ☐ I checked for capitals, periods, commas, and question marks.

Content

- ☐ I have a **HEADLINE** that names the story.
- ☐ I have a **BYLINE** that shows my name as the author.
- ☐ I have a **BEGINNING** that gives the most important facts.
- ☐ I have a **MIDDLE** part that tells details about the story.
- ☐ I have an **ENDING** that gives the reader an idea to remember.

Diorama Scene

A diorama is a small version of a real life scene. Create a diorama about a topic you are studying.

What you need:

Here are some materials that you might like to use to make your diorama:

- cardboard box, pizza box or shoe box
- found materials like yarn, or tissue paper rolls
- construction paper
- tissue paper,
- paint
- glue
- scissors

What you do:

STEP 1: Choose a diorama stage like a cardboard box or shoe box.

STEP 2: Paint or draw and colour a background for your diorama.

STEP 3: Use the diorama outlines to draw and colour things to help create your diorama. Add other details for your diorama using different materials.

STEP 4: Write about your diorama.

Diorama Outlines

Use these outlines to help create a diorama.

Diorama Outlines

Use these outlines to help create a diorama.

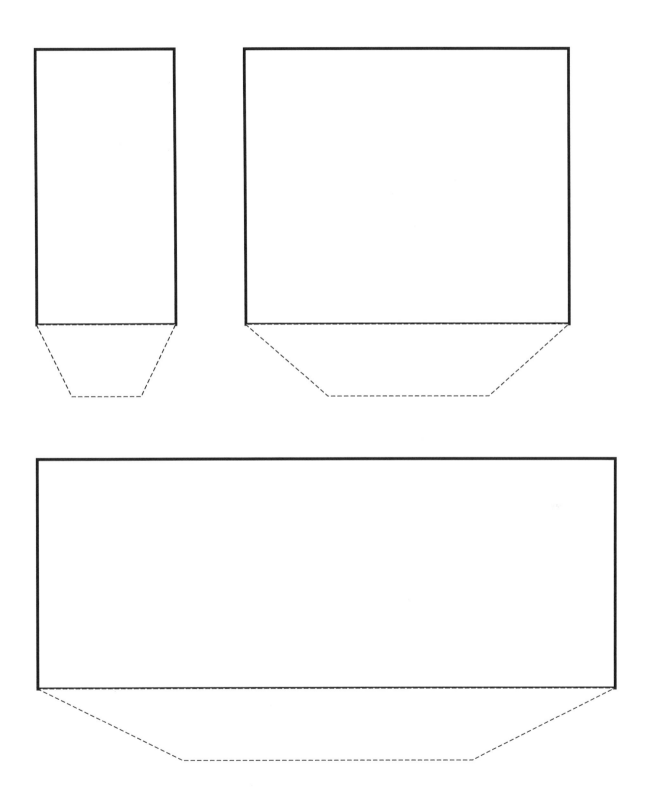

Seeing The Setting....

Draw a picture of a setting. Write about the time and place happening in your setting.

This is a setting of _____

A Word Search About

_____

Create a word search and share it with your classmates.

Word List

Thinking About My Work!

name _____

I am proud of _____

_____

I want to learn more about _____

_____

I need to work on _____

I will do better by _____

Thinking About My Work!

name _____

I am proud of _____

_____

I want to learn more about _____

_____

I need to work on _____

I will do better by _____

Map Making Checklist

name _____

Organization and Neatness
   • My work is neat and has details.
   • My features can be clearly read.
   • I have a title for my map.	

Map Legend • I have a complete map legend.	
Scale • The features are drawn to scale.	
Spelling • I checked for spelling.	

Map Making Checklist

name _____

Organization and Neatness
   • My work is neat and has details.
   • My features can be clearly read.
   • I have a title for my map.	

Map Legend • I have a complete map legend.	
Scale • The features are drawn to scale.	
Spelling • I checked for spelling.	

Map Making Rubric

Student name_____

	Level 1	Level 2	Level 3	Level 4
Organization and Neatness	Few of the labels or features can be clearly read.	Some of the labels or features can be clearly read.	Most of the labels or features can be clearly read.	All of the labels or features can be clearly read.
Map Legend	The legend is missing or difficult to read.	The legend contains an incomplete set of symbols.	The legend contains a set of symbols.	The legend contains a thorough set of symbols.
Scale	Less than half of the features on the map are drawn to scale.	More than half of the features on the map are drawn to scale.	Most of the features on the map are drawn to scale.	All of the features on the map are drawn to scale.
Spelling	Less than half of the words on the map are spelled correctly.	More than half of the words on the map are spelled correctly.	Most of the words on the map are spelled correctly.	All of the words on the map are spelled correctly.

Teacher Comments:

_____

_____

_____

_____

Student Participation Rubric

Level	Student Participation Descriptor
Level 4	Student consistently contributes to class discussions and activities by offering ideas and asking questions.
Level 3	Student usually contributes to class discussions and activities by offering ideas and asking questions.
Level 2	Student sometimes contributes to class discussions and activities by offering ideas and asking questions.
Level 1	Student rarely contributes to class discussions and activities by offering ideas and asking questions.

Understanding of Concepts Rubric

Level	Understanding of Concepts Descriptor
Level 4	Student shows a thorough understanding of all or almost all concepts and consistently gives appropriate and complete explanations independently. No teacher support is needed.
Level 3	Student shows a good understanding of most concepts and usually gives complete or nearly complete explanations. Infrequent teacher support is needed.
Level 2	Student shows a satisfactory understanding of most concepts and sometimes gives appropriate, but incomplete explanations. Teacher support is sometimes needed.
Level 1	Student shows little of understanding of concepts and rarely gives complete explanations. Intensive teacher support is needed.

Communication Of Concepts Rubric

Level	Communication of Concepts Descriptor
Level 4	Student consistently communicates with clarity and precision in written and oral work. Student consistently uses appropriate terminology and vocabulary.
Level 3	Student usually communicates with clarity and precision in written and oral work. Student usually uses appropriate terminology and vocabulary.
Level 2	Student sometimes communicates with clarity and precision in written and oral work. Student sometimes uses appropriate terminology and vocabulary.
Level 1	Student rarely communicates with clarity and precision in written and oral work. Student rarely uses appropriate terminology and vocabulary.

Class Evaluation List

Student Name	Class Participation	Understanding of Concepts	Communication of Concepts	Overall Evaluation

Social Studies Project Rubric

Student Name: _____

Project: _____

Criteria	Level One	Level Two	Level Three	Level Four
Content/Information • required information • accurate • supporting details	- limited information - few supporting details	- some of the required information - some supporting details	- most of the required information - accurate and complete supporting details	- comprehensive information - very thorough supporting details
Writing Conventions • spelling • grammar • punctuation	- spelling and grammar errors in good copy - inconsistent punctuation	- some spelling, grammar, and punctuation errors in good copy	- most of the spelling, grammar and punctuation is correct in good copy	- all spelling, grammar, and punctuation are correct in good copy
Graphics / Pictures • match information • colour enhanced	- pictures rarely match information - incomplete	- pictures partially match information - some pictures are incomplete	- pictures are complete and appropriate	- pictures are outstanding and consistently match information
Overall Presentation • neat • organization	- little organization or neatness	- some organization and neatness	- general organization and neatness	- outstanding organization and neatness

Teacher Comments:

Other Useful Websites

Canadian Geographic For Kids

http://www.canadiangeographic.ca/kidstest/

Four Directions Teaching

This is an amazing online audio and visual narrated that help students learn about the five diverse First Nations in Canada.

http://www.fourdirectionsteachings.com/

Backcheck: Hockey for Kids

learn about the early days of hockey, the French-Canadian hockey tradition, women's hockey, and more on this detailed site from the National Library of Canada.

http://www.nlc-bnc.ca/hockey/kids/

Wanted: Albertosaurus

On this site, learn all about the mysterious Albertosaurus fossils found in Alberta, Canada. From National Geographic.
http://www.nationalgeographic.com/ngkids/0005/dino/

Marketplace

Students will have an introduction to Canada's economy and how it works.

http://www.canadiangeographic.ca/cgkidsatlas/market.asp

The Middle Ages
This site will introduce children to life in the Middle Ages.

http://web.archive.org/web/20080303002517id_/http:/www.mnsu.edu/emuseum/history/middleages/

First Among Equals: Canadian Prime Ministers
On this site, students can play games and see pictures of Canada's Prime Ministers.

http://www.collectionscanada.ca/2/9/h9-5500-e.html

McMichael Art Gallery

Go to the kids' page and find an interactive activities area for kids. This site has a colouring book, as well as a wide range of interesting information written especially for kids about Canadian art.

http://www.mcmichael.com/

Social Studies Star!

———————————

GREAT WORK !

Quality Worker!

Way to go!

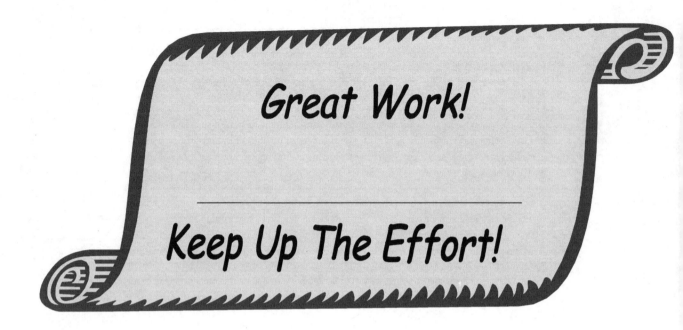